Discovering
Craft of the
Inland Waterways

SHIRE PUBLICATIONS LTD

Contents

Introduction	3
1. Early types of craft	5
2. State barges and similar craft	7
3. Hand-propelled craft	9
4. The Thames sailing barge	19
5. The Wey barge	26
6. The Norfolk keel	27
7. The Norfolk wherry	28
8. The Humber keel	29
9. Tom puddings	31
10. Trent barges	49
11. The Tyne keel	49
12. Puffers	50
13. Mersey and Weaver flats	52
14. Short boats	53
15. Severn trows	55
16. Severn tankers	57
17. Avon tar barges	57
18. Stroudwater barges	57
19. Teignmouth keels	58
20. Narrowboats	59
21. Steam narrowboats	66
22. Welsh narrowboats	67
23. Tub boats	68
24. Packet boats	68
25. Tugs	70
26. Dredgers	72
27. Icebreakers	73
28. General-service boats and flats	73
29. Inspection boats and launches	74
30. Pleasure steamers	75
31. Cabin cruisers and converted narrowboats	76
32. Ferries	77
33. Contemporary commercial craft	78
Glossary	80
Bibliography	84
Places to visit	85
Index	87

17. JUN. 1987

386·22

17. JUN. 1987

Introduction

The traditional British love of the sea and mastery of seamanship, on which the prosperity of a former empire depended, was at least partly fostered by navigation of the inland waterways. There are few parts of Britain remote from natural lakes and rivers, and the addition of a canal system during the second half of the eighteenth century added further dimensions. 'Messing about in boats' has passed through many phases from an essential means of communication, to the comparatively safe and cheap transport of merchandise, and finally to a great leisure industry.

This book is concerned with the types and development of various craft using the waterways of Britain from prehistoric times to the present day.

ACKNOWLEDGEMENTS

The cover illustration, a detail of 'Boulter's Lock, Sunday Afternoon 1895' by Edward J. Gregory, is in the Lady Lever Art Gallery, Port Sunlight, and is reproduced by permission of the National Museums and Galleries on Merseyside.

The publishers acknowledge the assistance of Mr Richard Hutchings. The line drawings are by the author. Photographs are acknowledged as follows: Keith Bennett, plates 7, 20, 21; British Waterways Board (photograph by Derek Pratt), plates 15, 23; George H. Haines, plate 19; Museum of the Royal Engineers, Chatham (photograph by Keith Bennett), plate 10; National Maritime Museum, plates 6, 8, 9, 13; Crown copyright, Science Museum, London, plates 1, 3, 4, 5, 11, 12, 16; Mrs P. M. Smith, plate 22: Michael E. Ware, plates 14, 17; M. Williams, plate 2; Wyre Forest Council, plate 18.

Fig. 1. Early dugout.

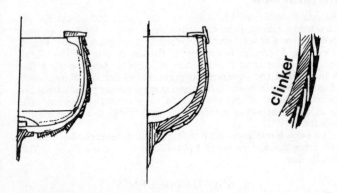

Fig. 2. Cross-sections of types of boat building: (from the left) clinker build; carvel build; and doubled build.

Fig. 3. Teifi coracle upended.

4

1. Early types of craft

The earliest forms of water-borne craft originated from raft and dugout, as used by primitive tribes in all parts of the inhabited world. It is probable that they were first used on inland waters such as placid lakes and less turbulent rivers, either to ferry people across or to catch fish and waterfowl. They may also have been used as a means of communication between the prehistoric lake dwellings that were built above shallow waters as a protection from wild beasts and hostile tribesmen.

A **raft** was obviously the first choice. The aim was to increase both the carrying space above the water level and improve buoyancy by lashing together sufficient numbers of logs to make a floating platform.

The same ends were also served by hacking or burning out the inner part of a fallen tree trunk to form a **dugout** which was easier to manage with pole or paddle. Though superior to the raft in speed and certain aspects of navigation, it lacked stability and was limited in carrying potential. Forms of dugout, however, appear to have been used for ferrying until the middle ages. It was from attempts to combine the more useful features of both raft and dugout that all forms of boats and ships eventually developed.

With both dugout and raft there were attempts at forming a prow, raising the sides (to keep out wash and waves) and, in the case of dugouts, introducing a keel that might assist in general stability. From the dugout may have developed the canoe, which is generally recognised as the earliest form of true boat. From the raft with raised sides and upturned ends developed the punt, ark, sampan and even the ocean-going junk.

The early civilisations of the Mediterranean and Middle East carvel-built their craft. They had an inner framework of ribs and keel, strengthened with thwarts and crossbeams, built up with side planks fitting edge to edge to create a smooth outer surface. With carvel build the structure was also drawn inwards towards the stern, a feature still present in canal boats and some river barges of the twentieth century. What is known as clinker build, better adapted to rougher northern waters, appears to have been favoured by the Scandinavians. This had overlapping side planks, making a series of longitudinal ledges running the length of the boat from stem to stern. The term *clinker* derives from the clinching of nails or driving them through planks.

In north-western Europe, skinboats were constructed on a light or woven framework. These were prevalent in Celtic countries, especially Britain and Ireland; the largest, known as the **Irish curragh,** was sturdy enough to weather the roughest Atlantic storms. Although mainly used for fishing and, to a lesser extent, for trading, they may have been used by early Celtic navigators for exploratory journeys across oceans.

While a type of smaller curragh was used on lakes and estuaries, the most popular skinboat for inland navigation, especially on swift-flowing rivers, was the **coracle**. This appeared in several different forms but was generally of a rounded or oval shape, although some were square-shaped and flattened out at the front. They were fairly widespread from East Anglia to West Wales, remaining in use in Wales and the Severn valley until the present century. A limited number are still made in Wales and on the banks of the Severn at Ironbridge, Salop.

The main types of coracle are the Teifi and Towy coracles of Wales, the Wye coracle and four versions of the Severn coracle, one of which (or a craft very similar) was also used on the Dee and in parts of North Wales. In appearance coracles resemble an open umbrella with a cross-seat almost amidships. Construction was of woven laths, either willow withies or hazel rods, covered with animal skins. Later they were covered with light cloth, canvas or calico, tarred and waterproofed. The laths of the framework varied with size and type, those on the Teifi having nine across and six lengthways, while many of the Severn craft had seven each way. A number had two diagonal laths, in the form of a Saint Andrew's cross, for greater stability. Nails were rarely used below the gunwale or upper line. A Teifi coracle was up to 72 inches long, with a maximum beam of 40 inches and 34 inches across the centre-seat, which gave it a slightly waisted appearance. The depth varied between 12 and 17 inches. The average weight was 30 pounds. The Severn coracle was slightly smaller and lighter than those used in West Wales.

The cross-seat of most coracles has a broad loop, band or cord, for portage. The boatman used a single paddle of oak or ash, about five feet long, while many coracles also carried a small boxwood fish club, known as a *priest*.

When not in use the coracle was kept under cover, leaning against a wall; it was rarely moored to the bank. It could be carried on the back from place to place, the band or strap slipping over back, chest and shoulders, leaving the boater's hands free for other gear such as fish nets and paddle.

The main use of the coracle, especially during later years, was in salmon-fishing or netting (nets of hemp and horsehair were trawled from two boats). It could also be used for ferrying, for gathering reeds and for river-dipping sheep, a practice widely followed in parts of Wales. It is now undergoing a limited revival amongst fly-fishermen. At Shrewsbury, where there is a sports ground near the river, a man with a coracle is often stationed on the bank to retrieve footballs kicked into the water.

2. State barges and similar craft

The name *barge* has several different meanings on the inland waterways. In general terms it is a flat-bottomed craft, but many people describe all inland trading craft as barges, including craft of the narrow canals, which are more correctly narrowboats or long boats. This is a matter of dimensions rather than purpose or construction, as the true barge tends to be broad in the beam and could not pass the locks and bridgeholes of the narrow waterways that form the greater part of the canal system. For reasons of economy, engineering works on many of the canals were gauged to a width of slightly over seven feet; river barges and those trading on the broad canals are wider than this, and broad canals are termed barge canals or navigations.

A number of passenger and pleasure craft have also been termed barges. A shore boat attached to a warship may be termed a barge, especially an admiral's barge used by senior officers. The college barges of Oxford, however, are more like houseboats and form the headquarters of rowing clubs connected with the university.

Passenger barges appear to have been either privately owned or related to state and civic ceremonial, and although used in all parts of the country they were mainly associated with the Thames and London, where they served royalty, noblemen and officers of state in much the same way as private coaches on the land. It is known that such vessels were also used on the Dee because the victorious Saxon king Edgar was rowed by eight vassal kings from his royal palace to the church of Saint John further downstream.

The Thames served London as its main thoroughfare and, long after the improvement of streets and road transport, a passage by water was both more direct and in every way more agreeable than jolting over cobbles, with the numerous traffic delays that were common from the seventeenth century onwards. Most great

Fig. 4. State barge, sixteenth century.

houses had their watergates and private landing places, and at intervals there were public steps from which watermen plied for hire with skiffs, gigs and other types of craft, not unlike modern cabbies.

Until the fifteenth century boats and barges on the Thames appear to have been propelled by poling, paddling or punting, rather than rowing. Use was also made, wherever possible, of towing from the banks (on the upper reaches) or sailing (on the broader, lower reaches). There was little rowing or sculling before John Norman, Lord Mayor of London in 1453, set a fashion for the use of private barges propelled by oars, which appears to have been copied by many leading citizens.

These private barges, not all of which were flat-bottomed, greatly encouraged the use and design of other pleasure craft like the Thames or pleasure wherry of V section and the Thames skiff or general-purpose rowing boat. As a result skill in rowing and handling small craft greatly increased, with races and contests such as the Doggett's Coat and Badge, named after the comedian

Fig. 5. College barges.

Thomas Doggett, a patron of aquatic sports.

The private **state barge,** usually higher at the poop than at the prow, was elaborately carved, painted, gilded, and decked with banners and pennants. About half its length might be covered by a roof or awning to shelter the passengers. Side windows or apertures would be protected by elaborate drapes. A trumpeter might stand in the bows to announce its arrival at a landing stage, while the helmsman would be seated in the stern on what resembled a gilded throne.

Long after the decline of boat and barge as regular means of passenger transport, the citizens of London were treated to elaborate pageants on the Thames, and music and picnic parties on the Thames and other rivers were fashionable amusements until the second half of the eighteenth century.

College barges

These were mainly static craft, used by the Oxford colleges, and were moored along the banks of the Isis. They were large, flat-bottomed vessels, approached by gangways, some having attached floats or landing stages on the river side. Many of the older ones, dating back well over a century and a half, were replaced by a prosaic form of houseboat. The more interesting survivors are now being restored. These had a high, flat stern and poop, similar to the popular concept of a galleon, and an extensive upper deck used as a promenade or grandstand, with flagpole well forward (sometimes mistaken for a mast). They had sash windows and gilded scrollwork, although most paintwork was black, white and cream.

---

3. Hand-propelled craft

There were numerous rowing clubs on the Thames from the late eighteenth century and during the Victorian era. The London watermen contended for the Doggett's Coat and Badge in rather clumsy craft with side strakes and fairly high sides or freeboard above water level, flaring upwards to the sill or bottom of the rowlocks. From the 1770s there was a fashion for racing in pair-oared boats or skiffs, which would have been seen in great numbers on London's river at that period. Most of the early rowing clubs had large heavy-duty boats of clinker build, designed for wholesome exercise rather than racing honours. These were bluff and fairly high above water level, even when crewed by an eight. Both eight- and ten-oared boats were raced, especially on the upper tidal reaches of the Thames, from about 1810. By 1811 Eton College had three eight-oared boats, two six-oared boats and one ten-oared boat.

In 1855 a keelless eight-oar boat for racing made its appearance on the Thames at Henley. This had been designed by Matthew Taylor for the Royal Chester Rowing Club. It was built on moulds, bottom side upwards, with an outer skin of bent or moulded cedarwood. Ribs were fitted inside the skin after the boat had been reversed. This was copied by Oxford University, who launched a similar craft of their own, 63 feet in length and 25 inches in beam, at Putney in 1857. Dimensions and fittings varied with the years but these were prototypes for most racing boats of the following century.

The modern eight-oared shell

This is the type used for over eighty years in the University Boat Race, crewed by a coxed eight. It is 62 feet long, 24 inches wide, and 10 inches deep. Hulls are made of cedarwood imported from Central America and only three sixteenths of an inch thick. Although seeming fragile, the shell, when travelling at an average speed of twelve miles per hour, has to withstand pressures of 8,000 pounds below the waterline. The keel and inwales or inner planks (strakes) below the gunwales are made from American pine, which has a smooth almost silken finish, and are held in place by ribs of English sycamore. Inner, diagonal braces are made of mahogany. The outer cover or planking is moulded over the ribs—after a process of heating and dampening—joined to the keel and inwales and laid in three sections on each side. The oars are held in place by outriggers of drawn steel tubing. Over 3,500 copper nails are used in making the average eight-oared shell, with a gross of screws for each crewman. The finished boat weighs about 280 pounds. During the 1970s experiments were made with fibreglass and other materials so the future for this type of craft appears to be with a moulded structure.

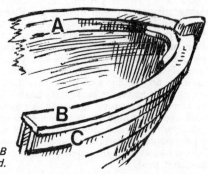

Fig. 6. A Inwale. B Gunwale. C Saxboard.

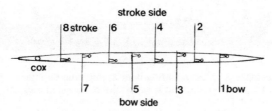

Fig. 7. Rowing positions of a coxed eight.

Other hand-propelled craft

Other popular racing boats dating from the middle of the nineteenth century included the **clinker eight,** similar to the eight-oared shell, although heavier, but with overlapping planks of clinker build. This craft was seldom over 60 feet long and could be as short as 56 feet. The beam or width was from 24 to 27 inches and the depth 8 to 9 inches.

The **clinker four** had a length of 38 to 42 feet, a beam of 23 to 24 inches and a depth of 8 to 9 inches.

The **outrigger pair,** its oars supported by full outriggers of drawn steel, so that the rowlocks were some distance from the sides of the boat, was either of clinker build or a shell. It was 30 to 34 feet long, with a beam of 14 to 16 inches and a depth of 7 to 8 inches.

The **outrigger scull** was propelled by a man using two sculls or short oars, one in each hand. (A person using a longer or true oar uses both hands on the same oar, there being alternately one oar on each side, a minimum of two oars being required to row any type of craft.) The outrigger affords better leverage than the inrigger, which has rowlocks above the gunwales. Outrigger sculls were 25 to 30 feet long, with a 10 to 13 inch beam, and 5½ to 6 inches deep.

Fig. 8. Gig.

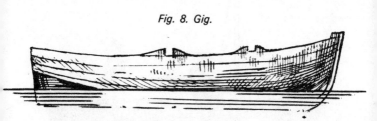

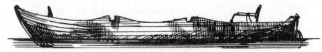

Fig. 9. Skiff.

The **gig** was an open rowing boat at one time popular on inland waterways and in harbours, especially on the Thames, although declining in popularity from the 1860s. It was of clinker build with a straight sheer or sides below the gunwales. On the Thames it outlived its ordinary usefulness, well into the twentieth century, for exercise and training purposes. The so called **coaching gig** was about 26 to 28 feet in length, with a 3 foot 4 inch beam, and 10½ to 14 inches deep. Many sea-going and estuarine craft carried a gig or small boat known as a **captain's gig** for the private use of the master.

The **skiff** was a popular pleasure boat, sometimes also used for ferry work. It was fairly light and eventually replaced the slower, heavier gig. The typical **Thames skiff,** used on the upper reaches of the river, had a pointed stem and what were termed high or 'extended' sides. The design varied slightly on different parts of the river, mainly in the angle of stem-rake, but dimensions averaged between 24 and 26 feet in length, between 3 feet 9 inches and 4 feet in beam and about 12 inches in depth. The **Eton skiff** was longer and narrower with a length of 27 feet, beam of 2 feet 3 inches and depth of 9½ inches. To confuse matters further, a light form of gig was known as a skiff, especially on the lower reaches of the Thames. A large clinker-built boat known as an **oyster skiff** was to be seen on the Essex rivers and estuaries. It was used mainly

Fig. 10. Oyster skiff.

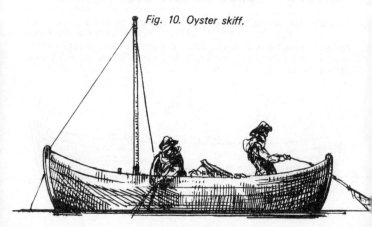

Fig. 11. Old Thames wherry.

—but not exclusively—in the oyster fisheries. It was frequently pointed at both ends or double-ended and might step a short mast, to be used either for rowing or sailing.

The **wherry** was a large open boat, originally used on broad rivers as a passenger ferry. It developed on East Anglian waterways as a general-purpose carrier; the Norfolk wherry, described later, was the most typical form. It varied in size and shape even more than skiffs, according to locality. The old **Thames wherry,** of which very few were to be seen after the First World War, was fairly long and wide with a high-pointed stem or *nose,* often sheathed in iron (an *iron-nose).* Some were pointed at both ends and could be rowed in either direction, usually manned by professional watermen. The larger types resembled pontoons.

The **whiff** was a narrow sculling boat used for racing or training, fitted with outriggers. It superseded the older type of wager boat and was in turn replaced by the best boat and modern shell. Mainly of clinker build, but light and handy, the average whiff was 20 to 23 feet long, 16 to 18 inches wide and 6 inches deep from keel to the top of the stem. A version known as the **whiff gig** was only 19 feet long but at least 2 feet 8 inches in the beam and 12 inches deep.

The **randan** was a development of the Thames wherry and also gave its name to the system by which it was propelled. This combined sculling and rowing in the same craft, for it had three hands and a cox. Stroke and bow were oarsmen, while the second

Fig. 12. Randan.

Fig. 13. Wager boat.

man sculled. This method of propulsion was widely used from the mid nineteenth century, for both speed and convenience, by customs officials, river police and members of the Thames Conservancy Board. A pleasure boat known as a randan was later introduced on the upper reaches of the Thames and other rivers. This was between 27 and 30 feet long, 4 to 4½ feet in the beam and 13 inches deep from keel to the top of the stempost.

A **best boat** was a superior type of craft used for sculling matches. It developed from the earlier **wager boat,** so called because heavy wagers were often laid on the events in which they appeared. Both types were made from the lightest possible materials with just sufficient room for a single occupant. Most best boats were of semicircular section, without a proper keel but with a type of fin placed aft of the sculler. The interior of the best boat was lined with waterproofed silk, there being a sliding seat and full outriggers.

A **rum-tum** was a form of whiff, with roughly the same dimensions, used for 'rum-tum races' on the Thames. It was originally used by rowing men unable to afford their own craft, especially the more expensive wager or best boats. Rum-tums were the property of a club and although fairly light and of standard design they were far from first-class racers. They were fitted with sliding seats and full outriggers. Rum-tum racing was introduced during the second half of the nineteenth century.

Fig. 14. Funny.

A **funny** was a narrow clinker-built boat, mainly used on the upper reaches of the Thames. It accommodated a single person either for sculling matches or for training purposes. It had full outriggers and double ends and was well pointed at bow and stern. It was fairly deep for its length.

The **hoy** was either a small boat acting as a tender, especially in rivers or estuaries, or a small coasting vessel under sail. The former type was a large rowing boat that ferried passengers to sea-going and estuarine vessels, especially where there was inadequate wharfage. There was also a small river or harbour lighter perhaps wrongly termed a hoy. Lightermen working and owning their own craft were often known as 'hoymen'.

The **long boat,** not to be confused with the West Country name for a canal narrowboat, was usually the longest and largest of several boats carried by a sea-going ship. It could be used, however, on tidal rivers and estuaries, propelled by ten oars, often doubled-banked. This meant that two rowers shared the same thwart or bench, 'bank' being a corruption of the French word for 'bench', *banc*.

The **peter-boat** was a Thames rowing or sailing boat used for fishing, decked fore and aft. It was clinker-built, double-ended and of sturdy construction. Different versions were used for catching fish above and below London Bridge; they were known as the 'above-bridge' and 'below-bridge' types. Those found above the bridge were slightly smaller than the more popular estuarine craft. They were named after Saint Peter, the patron saint of fishermen. It is thought that this type of craft was originally used in the Baltic and by offshore fishermen in Norway and other Scandinavian countries, especially for training young men apprenticed to the fishing fleets. They were up to 25 feet long and 6 feet beam, of variable depth. Some of the above-bridge types were only about 14 feet long. Peter-boats had a well or hold amidships in which to store the catch.

Fig. 15. Small peter-boat.

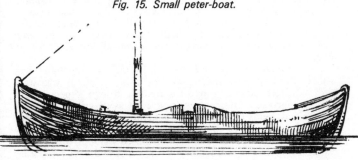

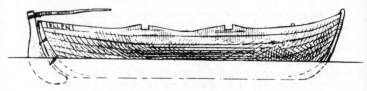

Fig. 16. Medway doble.

Another popular fishing boat of the lower reaches of the Thames, seldom seen above Gravesend, was the **bawley.** This could be rowed but was essentially a sailing vessel or smack, used for shrimping or catching whitebait. It was cutter-rigged, having a trysail or mainsail without a boom. Although an interesting craft worthy of record, belonging to the same family as the peter-boat and Medway doble, it is not within the true definition of a hand-propelled craft.

The general-purpose and fishing boat of the Medway was the **Medway doble,** a few of which are still in use, although fitted with auxiliary motors since the 1930s. Like the peter-boat it could be used with oars or sails and was similar at both ends. Some, used mainly for sailing, had deep centre boards. They were about 12 feet long, 4 feet 3 inches in the beam and 17 inches deep. Those used for fishing had a wet well amidships, this being a tank in which to keep the catch alive until landing. A narrow space on either side of the well was used for stowing nets and other gear. Early types used drift nets while later craft used the beam trawl.

A **dinghy** was a small open boat towed by a yacht or launch to be used as a tender. Also known as a 'pram' or 'punt', it was sometimes flat-bottomed and blunt- or swim-ended, fairly safe for children and the older novice learning to handle a boat. In recent years many have been fitted with outboard motors, while others are rigged for sailing and racing. The average dinghy, more a type than a specific craft, is of strong but squat appearance. Although originally clinker-built, recent versions are smooth-sided, constructed of fibreglass, marine plywood or any other suitable materials. The modern sailing dinghy appears in over two hundred types found in different parts of the world, all under 20 feet in length.

The **pontoon** derived from the early dugout canoe and was usually flat-bottomed and square- or swim-ended. It was used both as a ferry and to support a floating bridge, especially for military purposes. Of great antiquity, it was described by Julius Caesar and Aulus Gellius. It was generally considered a portable boat but needed to be conveyed on a truck or carriage drawn by draught animals. Pontoon trains were used in both world wars, especially by the Royal Engineers in the construction of temporary bridges, and later inspired the development of the Mulberry harbour.

The **punt** is a flat-bottomed boat usually, but not always, propelled by a pole or *quant*. The term *quant* is used mainly in East Anglia and the Fens. This craft derived from the pontoon and dugout of ancient times. The original or **rough punt** was used for fishing on inland lakes and backwaters; able to move slowly through still waters without too much wash or disturbance, it had ample space for fishing gear. About the middle of the nineteenth century punts became popular for pleasure purposes and eventually for racing. A lighter, more elegant type emerged at this period, with greater overhang of the swim-ends. Those for racing could be propelled at almost incredible speeds, the serious art of punting being much harder than it at first appears. Some punts were also propelled by sculls or paddles, while a few stepped a single mast and carried sail. The **racing punt** was about 30 feet long, 18 inches in the beam and 6 to 7 inches deep. Some, however, were up to 35 feet, although the more popular **semi-racer** was between 28 and 30 feet long, 2 feet in the beam and 9½ inches deep. The modern **pleasure punt** is 26 to 28 feet long, 33 inches in the beam and 12 to 14 inches deep.

The **gun punt** or **duck punt** was a type of shallow flat-bottomed craft pointed at each end and covered over at bow and stern. It was usually propelled by means of a paddle but could also step a mast for sailing. Used for the once fashionable sport of punt-gunning or wildfowling, it was confined to the marshes, estuaries and rivers of the eastern counties, especially near the Wash. The fore part of

Fig. 17. Dinghy, old style.

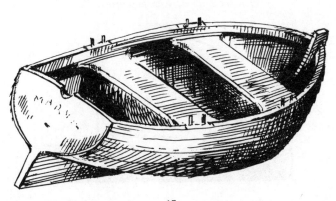

Fig. 18. Gun punt, or duck punt.

the gun punt, shaped not unlike an Eskimo canoe or kayak of Greenland, supported the long barrel of a muzzle-loading cannon used for shooting waterfowl including geese, teal and shellduck. The single occupant was the gunner dressed in a white smock and cap, firing at rising game birds from a distance of between eighty and a hundred yards. A near approach was mainly successful in rough weather and only a few shots could be fired within a space of several hours. For many gunners a single shot in a day would be enough, as this might kill as many as fifty birds. The craft, however, was difficult to control and easy to capsize, its navigation fraught with dangers and discomforts.

Trows, not to be confused with the larger sailing craft mentioned later, were a form of double boat used on the Tyne for salmon-fishing and netting.

As in the coracle fishing of Wales and the west Midlands, the theory was to lower the nets between two similar craft. The trow, in this case, was often a much used clinker-built boat, the hull 'doubled' with extra planking on the outside fitting below the overlap of the original planks. This gave the boat the appearance of a carvel-built type. There were very few trows after the mid nineteenth century, mainly owing to increased coal traffic and industrial pollution of the Tyne.

Fig. 19. Canoe rig with battened sails.

The **canoe,** in modern terms, is any type of double-ended craft, often fairly high at stem and stern, designed to be propelled by paddles. It is a portable craft, mainly confined to inland waters, and is of shallow draught. Although the distant prototype may have been a hollowed-out log pointed at both ends, it was eventually constructed on a light framework covered by wood bark or animal skins. Some later types have been provided with masts for racing, there being a special canoe rig with battened sails, as used on the junks and river sampans of the Far East. A type of American or Red Indian canoe has been evident on the lakes of pleasure parks since the 1950s, gaining in popularity over pleasure punts and boats used for rowing or sculling. On still waters and within a confined space they are ideal for even the unskilled novice. Specially constructed canoes, covered in fore and aft, are used for negotiating rapids and racing, which make exciting sporting events. Some have even been used at sea, as are the native canoes of Greenland and the far north.

---

4. The Thames sailing barge

Perhaps the most characteristic and interesting craft on the inland waterways was the sailing barge that plied on the Thames and the Medway, although frequently trading with east-coast ports and able to cross the North Sea. It was greatly admired for the beauty of its reddish-brown sails, the mast and tackle of which could be lowered for passing under bridges. Although a picturesque vessel, it appeared less attractive without its sails and descended from an ugly box-shaped craft of a type once familiar in most harbours and estuaries of western Europe.

At this point it is necessary to examine the use and origins of the Thames barge. The river was navigable to sea-going trading vessels from the time of the Roman occupation and, throughout its history, London has always been a great port. As ships increased in size, however, there was the disadvantage of stranding large vessels on mud flats at low water, so from the late middle ages foreign-going shipping was mainly confined to the pool below London Bridge. Here many were unloaded in midstream and their cargoes were transferred to barges or lighters that would take them either to the nearest wharf or further up river. The lighter or dumb barge (the first name is derived from the lightening of cargo from other craft) was managed by a single man who punted or poled but later made use of large oars or sweeps. Taking advantage of the current and flow of the river and of the incoming tide, an experienced lighterman would manage his clumsy charge with great skill, at least for short distances. For over five centuries the expense and difficulty of constructing a system of docks or basins encouraged the discharging of cargo in midstream.

Goods to be taken further inland or to towns on the tributaries of the Thames were transferred to even larger craft that could proceed under their own sail, although sometimes hauled from the banks by gangs of men (bow-hauling) or teams of horses. This particularly applied to the so called **western barges,** which made beyond the tidal reaches, where shallows were often encountered and even flat-bottomed craft had to be towed into deeper waters, especially when becalmed on a sheltered reach. The Thames sailing barge, travelling fairly long distances under its own power, was soon acknowledged as a superior type of vessel but had much in common with the lighter, at least until the end of the eighteenth century. The first designs were swim-ended or swim-headed, similar to the lighter and much smaller punt, often known as a **swimmie.** This meant that the flat square ends of the barge or lighter were raked outwards to overhang water level, while the sides were fairly flat and straight. At the stern end, under the

Fig. 20. Thames barge, swim-headed type.

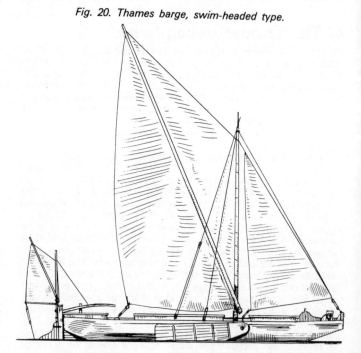

Fig. 21. Early Thames barge, 1640.

projection or swim, was an upright fin of metal or wood known as the *budget*. This kept the vessel on course and it was to this projection on a sailing barge that the rudder was fixed. Neither barge nor lighter was decked over, apart from a small foredeck which, in the case of a sailing barge, had a windlass for hauling up the anchor and raising the mast.

The barge usually had a living cabin or *cuddy* in the after part and was occasionally a family boat. The crew usually consisted of two or three men, although barges were frequently worked by a man and a boy, often with a dog to share their discomforts.

The tall mast was placed well forward, especially on the early types. Some sketches and prints, dating back to the seventeenth century, showed the mast before the carrying space and deck cargo. The lower part of the mast was stepped in a box-like structure, known as a *tabernacle,* from which it could be lowered and raised to pass under fixed bridges. For many years the only standing rigging was a forestay or rope from the prow to the masthead. From the mid eighteenth century, however, this was supplemented by a pair of side stays or shrouds.

The sail was large and square, trimmed by sheets (ropes) and braces connecting the yardarm to the sides of the vessel along the gunwales. This was closely akin to the square rig used by Viking raiders for their dragon or long ships, from which it may have descended, being popular with many types of craft along the east coast, where Vikings raided and finally settled. The sail was first hoisted up the mast by means of a centre rope or chain known as a *halyard,* later assisted by side ropes nearer the yard ends known as *lifts.* The lowered mast, in the early type, could be raised by hauling on the forestay. Such a barge could only sail with the prevailing wind and otherwise depended on sweeps, poling or towing.

The smaller barges drew only 16 inches but even these would be stranded in dry weather, especially when moving upstream towards Oxford, a trade that appears to have been established before the Norman conquest. In the course of time, however, flash locks or weirs were constructed at intervals on the upper reaches; from them water could be released to float off a stranded barge, but even these were not always effective. In times of prolonged drought the flat-bottomed barge was beyond the aid of manpower or even sudden flushes or flashes of water and had to remain in one spot for several days or weeks. A further impediment on the upper reaches was the excessive growth of weeds. These were seldom cut in large numbers as, although reducing the fairway, they were supposed to hold up the level of water, especially in time of drought. Dredging and scouring, even by the primitive methods of spooning, were greatly neglected, governed — as in many things — by mingled lassitude and superstition.

Barges working upstream at this period were limited to about 70 tons but those on the lower reaches may have been up to 146 tons. Towing paths were mainly neglected or non-existent and during the seventeenth century as many as twelve horses would be needed for the slow passage of a single western barge. Those with a second or smaller barge in tow needed seventeen or eighteen horses. The massive and strongly made towing ropes lasted for only a few voyages in each direction and cost the bargee between £10 and £12, which in those days was fairly expensive. By the 1760s there were nearly one hundred barges navigating from London docks in the westward trade alone, very few reaching below Deptford. There were even larger numbers connecting with the estuary and Medway ports. About half the barges were over 100 tons, but the larger types were restricted to the lower reaches. They were marked for a draught of 3 feet 9 inches fully loaded and allowed an inch in excess, but they could seldom find extra water for a through passage inland, at least not in summertime.

A few swim-headed barges were used on the Thames until the early 1930s. Most were concerned with general cargoes, but some specialised in carrying hay, straw, coal or fishmeal. A typical Medway barge with swim-ends was known as a **chalk barge,** used in traffic to and from the Kentish chalk quarries and from wharves near Gravesend. A typical feature of this barge and of others likely to encounter choppy water in the estuary was the use of triangular leeboards, which could be lowered from either side of the craft in the form of a stabiliser or keel.

During the late eighteenth century many barges were still swim-headed but with the ends proportionally narrower and the sides curved rather than straight. While many barges were open to the

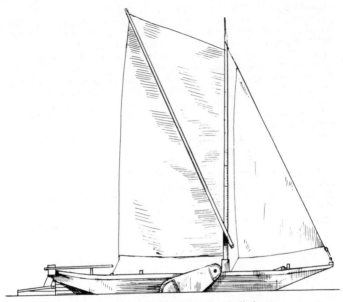

Fig. 22. Thames and Medway chalk barge.

sky, later types had their cargo space protected by covered hatches. The original square sail was eventually replaced by a spritsail.

The spritsail, so familiar on later Thames barges, derived its name from an Anglo-Saxon word meaning to sprout or poke out, which also relates to the even more familiar bowsprit. The sail was supported on a diagonal pole, extending its canvas to a high peak. The lower end or heel of the sprit was fixed to a metal band or snotter, suspended either by a rope from the masthead or by an iron ring or grommet. At the upper end the head of the sprit fitted into a cringle or loop, which set it tighter or looser as the snotter was elevated on the mast. This type of rig was useful when the spritsail was enclosed by brails or ropes, for gathering up and furling, ideal in the management of a craft either single-handed or undermanned. The sprit was usually much higher than the mast even when set at its usual angle of about 62 degrees. Spritsails were used in conjunction with foresails, while later barges, especially those for coastal or sea-going trade, made use of topsail and gib sails. Even the ordinary river barge of the Thames and the Medway sometimes had a mizzen sail and mast, either attached to

23

or working with the broad-bladed rudder.

During the early nineteenth century on the Thames and the Medway there were a number of squat, round-fronted or bowed **luff barges,** which challenged but did not replace the swim-headed types. Many of these had Irish skippers. The modern sailing barge with a vertical stem post was not widely accepted until the 1860s. Great encouragement was given to the improvement in design and upkeep of barges from this period by the introduction of annual sailing races on the Thames and the Medway. In later years several Thames barges were converted into pleasure craft and sailing them became a fashionable cult in maritime circles. There were a few in regular service until the early 1960s but those remaining are now kept for cruising or are the responsibility of preservation groups.

The original barges were of wood throughout. The keel, no part of which projected below the almost square-cornered (chine-built), flat-bottomed hull, was of English elm, although a longitudinal timber keelson, or inner keel, was made of Oregon pine. Stern and stem posts were of English oak and the bottom planks of Oregon

Fig. 23. Thames barge, spritsail type.

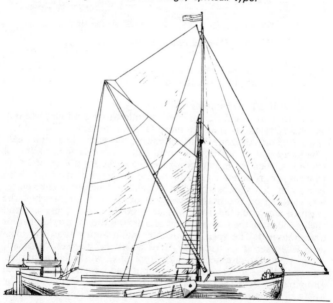

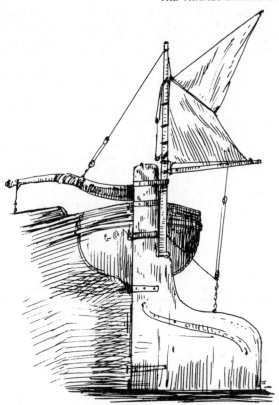

Fig. 24. Mizzen mast and sail on barge rudder head.

pine. The inner surface of the planking was sheathed in pinewood shearings laid over a coating of tar and cow-hair. Outer strakes were of elm. The rudder and leeboards were of oak, while the rudder blade was sometimes of pitch pine and the sprit of Oregon pine or red pine. Leading dimensions of the later spritsail barge were 82 feet long by 18 feet beam by 6½ feet deep (an average type from the mid 1860s). When fully loaded the gunwale was only a few inches above water level. The main mast was 33 feet high in the hoist, while an additional top mast for topsail rig would be 26 feet with a pole of 5 feet. The sprit might be about 56 feet.

25

From the 1850s a few iron barges were constructed, although the first of these were sheathed in wood. Later types were made of steel and even fitted with diesel engines. Two of the largest sailing barges ever used on the Thames were built at Brightlingsea in 1924; known as the *Aidie* and the *Barbara Jean,* each carried a cargo of about 260 tons and was of 119 tons tare or net weight. Both were lost in the Dunkirk operations of 1940, when coastal and estuarine craft of all types were called out to attempt the rescue of units of the British and allied armies, trapped by a German offensive, on the Normandy beaches. The modern barge is steered by a wheel rather than a tiller.

Other popular barges on the Thames included **stumpy barges,** swim-headed and only 45 to 55 feet long, used during the first half of the nineteenth century. The **stackie barge,** also swim-headed, often carried hay in her hold rising as much as 13 feet above deck level and appears to have been designed for the hay and straw traffic. They were of fairly shallow draught and could sail into riverside creeks, almost into the hay fields, to take on their cargoes, which were especially welcomed in London during the days of horse traffic. Very few were seen, however, after the decline of horse traffic in the 1920s. The mate or crewman of a stackie barge was often perched on top of the cargo, which resembled a floating haystack, and shouted directions to the helmsman. The last Thames barge in active service retired in 1971.

5. The Wey barge

This was a bluff-bowed, flat-bottomed barge operating mainly on the Wey Navigation and appearing in the London docks. It was a strongly built wooden craft in carvel style, having a D-shaped stern or transom. It was mainly towed by horses (two horses to a single barge), but in later years by tugs. Maximum beam was 13 feet 10½ inches and capacity 80 tons. It was built in the yards of Messrs Stevens of Guildford, owners of the Wey Navigation; the same type was constructed by them for over a century. The last Wey barge was launched in 1940, during the Second World War. A novel feature was the way in which the large rudder could fold back against the stern, to save space in locks and basins. The last working barge was used between London docks and a wharf at Coxes Lock Mill in 1969. Horse towing continued on the Wey until 1960. Several Wey barges have been preserved as pleasure craft and houseboats. Similar craft were also used on the now mainly waterless Basingstoke Canal, between a junction with the river Wey and Basingstoke.

6. The Norfolk keel

The Norfolk keel was a type of trading barge seen on East Anglian waterways before the more familiar Norfolk wherry, although not covering such a wide area. The earliest type was transom- or flat-ended, with D-shaped stern, but many later types were pointed at both ends or double-ended. Although popular during the seventeenth and eighteenth centuries they were reported 'very rare' by the middle of the nineteenth century and almost extinct by the late 1870s, being replaced by the wherry. The last Norfolk keel in regular trade survived until the 1890s, working from Norwich. After several years as a hulk or derelict she was sunk in the river Yare, between Brundall Gardens and Whitlingham, to mark the channel. In 1912, however, she was rescued for a short period by staff of the Science Museum, South Kensington, who recorded details and dimensions for the construction of an accurate display model.

Although most later types were double-ended, the sole survivor appears to have had a small transom stern. The cabin was in the fore part of the craft rather than the stern, while the cargo space was without covered hatches. The single mast, carrying a large sail, was amidships, stepped in a tabernacle but also secured by crosswise deck beams. The average Norfolk keel was much sturdier but far less elegant than the Norfolk wherry and likely to be much slower under sail. The hull was of clinker build and had an average length of 54 feet with a 14 foot beam. The depth was 4 feet, drawing slightly less than 4 feet of water. Cargo capacity was between 30 and 40 tons.

Fig. 25. Norfolk keel.

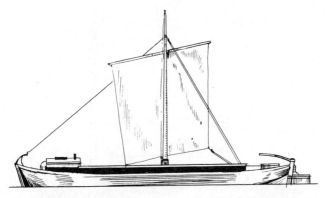

7. The Norfolk wherry

This was a general term for a type of flat-bottomed sailing barge of East Anglia, appearing in several different sizes and loading to a wide range of cargoes between 20 and 83 tons. They mainly worked inland from the ports of Yarmouth and Lowestoft, especially over the rivers Bure, Ant, Waveney and Yare, frequently appearing on the Norfolk Broads.

The hull was clinker-built, pointed at bow and stern; the gunwales were fairly close to the waterline and there was not much freeboard even when empty. The bows had a characteristic decoration in the form of an 'eye' or patch of white paint, which gave the optical illusion of a transom stern when viewed from a certain angle. The Norfolk wherry was a single-masted craft and carried a single sail, the prototype of una rig which was associated with broad-beamed sailing vessels along the east coast for many years. The peak of the sail could be set at a great height in order to collect as much wind as possible when sailing inland through places sheltered by tall trees. Although lacking a topsail and depending on a single gaffsail (a sail supported by a diagonal spar similar to the sprit of a Thames or Medway sailing barge), the

Fig. 26. Norfolk wherry.

wherry caught as much wind and displayed as great a spread of canvas as many larger vessels. Unlike the Thames barge, which frequently ventured into coastal waters and the North Sea, the wherry was only considered seaworthy—beyond the estuaries—in very calm weather. The mast was stepped in a tabernacle in which it could be lowered and raised for passing under obstructions. There were no shrouds or items of standing rigging, the only support being a forestay, which also served as a fall for lowering the mast.

Wherries have been working in East Anglia, where they were a popular form of general carrier, for at least three centuries but may have descended from an even earlier flat-bottomed ferry boat. The Thames wherry was a large rowing boat used for ferrying purposes. In later years the Norfolk wherry was often fitted with an auxiliary diesel engine. There are also records of steam wherries used during the 1880s and 1890s. One of the last wherries in regular commercial use (1960s) was the *Lord Roberts*, employed in seasonal sugar-beet traffic.

Small wherries were about 30 feet long with 9 foot beam, drawing 3 feet 3 inches when fully rigged and loaded. The largest known vessel of this type was the *Wonder* of Norwich, with dimensions of 65 feet by 19 feet and 7 foot draught. The mast, weighted at the bottom or heel with several hundredweights of lead, was 45 feet high, while the gaff was 30 feet, supporting about 500 square feet of canvas. The hold between mast and cabin (the cabin being placed well forward), was protected by up to twelve wooden hatches or hatch covers. On either side of the tiny cabin aft was a narrow area of decking used for poling or punting the vessel with the aid of a Norfolk barge pole or quant. This was often done in harbours to bring the craft up to her moorings.

A preserved Norfolk wherry is the 40 ton *Albion,* constructed in 1898 and now in the care of the Norfolk Wherry Trust. Many assert that this is the only authentic craft of its type still in existence.

---

8. The Humber keel

The Humber keel was a flat-bottomed, double-ended barge used on the Yorkshire Ouse, Humber and connected waterways and was sometimes known as a Yorkshire keel. It was rigged with a single mast, a little forward of midships, and usually carried a square sail, often with an additional topsail. Of carvel build, it had leeboards on either side and strong, bluff bows. The mast was stepped in a deep tabernacle in which it could be lowered or raised for passing under fixed bridges. The area of the hull below the waterline was usually dressed with tar, while the upper works were

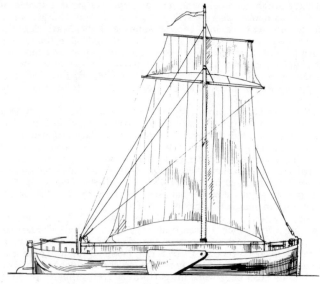

Fig. 27. Humber keel.

painted in light colours and frequently varnished. It measured 58 feet long and was 14 feet 6 inches in the beam and 6 feet to 6 feet 9 inches in draught. It had a capacity between 90 and 100 tons. Some craft have been recorded with up to 8 foot draught.

This type of keel has been in use for several centuries and is in direct descent from the long ships of the Viking raiders. They had the reputation of sailing close to the wind and were easy to handle, sometimes in the charge of a single man, although often family boats. During the 1890s there were at least 150 keels working on the Humber and Yorkshire Ouse from Hull to York. Numbers gradually diminished from the period of the First World War, although the last sailing keel was not withdrawn until 1949.

A slightly smaller version of the Yorkshire keel known as the **west country vessel** plied mainly on the Calder and Hebble Navigation and even further inland. They were often wooden horse barges, although they sometimes worked down the estuary to Hull, towed from Goole by steam tugs. At one time there was a considerable traffic in paving stones between Brighouse and Hull, some of the craft being operated by the Mellor family which had interests in a local quarry. Many of the stone slabs were

30

transhipped to coasters in Hull docks and sent to London. Return loads included grain, animal feeding-stuffs and raw materials. Later types were steel-hulled and fitted with diesel engines, although some were towed, above Goole, by tugs of the Calder Carrying Company. At one time bow hauling was more popular than horse hauling and where horses were used these were hired to the master of the keel rather than owned by him. A fleet of steel-hulled power-driven keels still works on the Sheffield and South Yorkshire Canal and connecting waterways, at least seventy owned by E. V. Waddington and Company of Swinton.

The older type of keel was noted for its carved and painted decorations in the form of grapevines and for a tall wooden stovepipe above a cabin at the fore end.

9. Tom puddings

Tom puddings are almost square steel compartment boats used on the Aire and Calder Navigations. They are hauled in trains by power-boats, formerly steam tugs but later diesels, rounded at bow and stern. The system was invented by W. H. Bartholomew, then

Fig. 28. Tom puddings and tug.

serving as engineer to the Aire and Calder Company. It first operated for the bulk transport of coal in 1865. The origin of the name is uncertain but may relate to the way in which compartments resemble oblong or square pudding tins. They have also been termed 'puddens' or even 'pans'.

William Bartholomew is an unsung hero of the canals as his invention brought new life to the port of Goole, which he helped to make an important outlet for the Yorkshire coalfields. Although traffic declined after the First World War, up to 1914 over a thousand Tom puddings were carrying one and a half million tons of coal per year.

The boats were originally of wood, reinforced with ironwork, but soon of all-steel construction, and first intended to be pushed or punted by the power-boat in batches of eleven. While trains of eleven or fewer Tom puddings were still propelled until the early 1920s, the majority were eventually towed astern in trains of between fifteen and twenty, although sometimes as many as thirty-two. The locks between Leeds, Wakefield and Goole are few and they are able to take six compartment boats at a time. The dimensions of each boat are 20 feet long, 16 feet beam, loading 35 tons to a draught of 6 feet.

The first compartment boats—designed for pushing—were connected and steered by means of steel ropes passing along the sides of each craft to winches on the power-boat. The boats were otherwise coupled together by central knuckle joints or posts fitting into a hollow stern post of the boat directly ahead. There was a gangway or catwalk covering the left-hand side of each compartment so that it was possible to walk from one end of the train to the other. Each boat, as a single unit, could be moved both vertically and laterally.

The first boat in each train, either towed or pushed, is attached to a false bow or **jebus,** sometimes known as a **dummy** or **dummy bows,** which is a small, separate and wedge-shaped craft. This helps to cleave the water and, in towing, keeps wash from the screw of the tug from slopping into the compartment, usually loaded very near the waterline. A jebus is sometimes attached to the front of the tug.

On arriving at Goole docks the compartments are detached from each other and their contents tipped—by means of cradle, hoist and chute — into the holds of sea-going colliers. Before the Second World War there were still over a thousand in everyday use but the number has now dropped below five hundred, many of which are kept in reserve. This is partly due to the introduction of other forms of transport and the discovery of North Sea gas.

A similar system, using a pusher tug, was also employed on the Birmingham Canal Navigations. The special steel boats designed for this purpose, with double ends, were long and narrow, and not unlike the traditional day boat of the area, described later. The tug,

1. The Lord Mayor of London's state barge, a model at the Science Museum.

2. A college barge moored at Oxford. These craft serve as the headquarters of university rowing clubs.

3. Thames wherry, a model at the Science Museum. The high-pointed stem or nose was often sheathed in iron.

4. Medway doble, a model at the Science Museum. These were the general-purpose and fishing boats of the Medway and could be propelled by oars or sails.

5. Thames peter-boat of the below-bridge type, a model at the Science Museum. Peter-boats used above London Bridge were smaller than the more popular estuarine fishing boat shown here.

6. Thames bawley. This type of fishing boat of the lower Thames estuary could also be propelled by oars.

7. *Pleasure punts for hire on the Cam at Cambridge. Punts became popular pleasure boats from the mid nineteenth century.*

8. The spritsail barge 'Alarm' on the river Thames.

9. Champion Thames barge, 1900.

10. *Military pontoon on its carriage at the Museum of the Royal Engineers at Chatham.*

11. *Norfolk keel, a Science Museum model. These East Anglian trading vessels tended to be superseded by the Norfolk wherry.*

12. *Norfolk wherry, a Science Museum model. These were flat-bottomed craft, working inland from Yarmouth and Lowestoft along the rivers and the Broads.*

13. Humber keel, also known as a Yorkshire keel. Direct descendants of the Viking long ships, these boats operated on the Humber and Yorkshire Ouse.

14. Tom puddings towed by a steam tug, c. 1900. Note the jebus or false bow in front of the Tom puddings.

15. Commercial craft on the Trent Navigation.

16. Model of the hull of a Tyne keel, at the Science Museum.

17. Severn trows loading from a sea-going ship in Gloucester Docks, c. 1900.

18. Day boat on the Staffordshire and Worcestershire Canal, 1900.
This type of narrowboat usually worked on day trips and so had only
a small cabin at the stern.

19. In the Waterways Museum at Stoke Bruerne is this mock-up of the cabin of a narrowboat decorated in traditional style.

20. The narrowboat 'Towcester' selling coal at a wharf on the Gloucester and Sharpness Canal in 1975.

21. The canal tug 'Speedwell' at Gloucester Docks in 1975. Once a steamer but now diesel-powered, she is used on the Gloucester and Sharpness Canal.

22. Vehicle and passenger ferry on the Severn at Hampton Loade, Salop, 1930.

23. Modern push-pull tug on the Sheffield and South Yorkshire Navigation.

little more than a floating engine about 14 feet long, had a notch on the bows that locked into the upright stern post of the boat to be pushed. The unit was kept rigid by means of wires and winches, as with the Tom puddings.

10. Trent barges

At one time large numbers of Yorkshire or Humber keels plied over the Trent Navigation. A few of the modern steel versions with diesel engines are still engaged in this trade, also a number of specially built estuarine and sea-going craft mainly concerned with the carriage of grain, bulk liquids and general merchandise. The latter are mostly steel-hulled barges with high bluff bows and counter sterns, a sizable fleet being owned by British Waterways. They are further noted for having large and fairly tall wheelhouses at the stern end, with living quarters at both ends of the central cargo space. A connection is made from the Humber ports as far inland as Nottingham with an entry to the commercially active Sheffield and South Yorkshire Canal at Keadby, about ten miles south of Trent Falls (the junction of Trent, Yorkshire Ouse and Humber). The average Trent barge is of about 400 tons capacity. Craft of 740 tons can reach Gainsborough, while 400 tons is the limit at Newark and 250 tons to Nottingham. There are extensive grain-storage facilities at Newark.

11. The Tyne keel

Similar to the Yorkshire or Humber keel but likely to be much smaller, the Tyne keel was used mainly in the Tyne coal trade to bring cargoes from the staithes or collieries inland to the sea-going colliers in the estuary. They ran a shuttle service, not unlike Thames lighters, depending not only on sails and oars but also on tide and current. They usually came down with the ebb tide and went upstream on the flood tide or flow.

The coal trade between the Tyne and London goes back to the middle ages, at least to the mid fourteenth century. Even in those days it was impossible for the larger sea-going colliers to reach the inland staithes, then known as *dykes*. Keels, already in use for other purposes, made ideal tenders and were used as such until the second decade of the twentieth century. Later types were of carvel build but the original Tyne keel was clinker-built, pointed at both ends and obviously descended from much earlier vessels of the Norsemen. From the mid nineteenth century many Tyne keels were replaced by larger clinker-built craft towed in trains by tugs

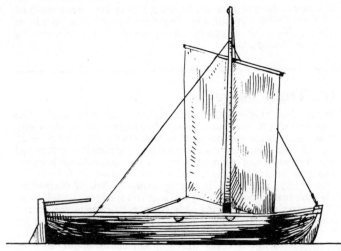

Fig. 29. Tyne keel.

and known as **Tyne wherries.** Very few were built after the 1860s although a number of keels survived until the period of the First World War. The last was reported on active duties in 1924 but seems to have been an isolated example.

The plan of the Tyne keel was almost oval, but pointed at both ends. Length was 42 feet and beam 19 feet; the load was 21 tons of coal in an outward direction. Fully loaded and rigged the craft drew 4 feet 6 inches of water. The single mast, rigged with a large square sail, was fitted into a tabernacle, slightly forward of the cargo space. There were small covered or decked areas fore and aft and a cabin or cuddy in the stern, known locally as a *hudduck*. Although some of the later types had a rudder, the majority were steered with a long oar known as a *swape* or sweep. The cabin could only be reached through a deck hatch and was of very limited headroom.

12. Puffers

These were Scottish steamers, sometimes known as coal gabbarts, now extinct apart from an example restored for preservation and occasional use. They operated mainly on the river Clyde but also on many of the firths and sea lochs round the west coast of Scotland, making extensive use of the Crinan Canal (thus avoiding a lengthy and dangerous passage round the Isle of Arran and Mull of Kintyre). They were mainly coal boats but could also be used for general merchandise, including livestock. Being flat-bottomed they could unload on any beach or mudflat at low water, frequently surrounded by carts, trucks and even hand-barrows of the local country folk. A considerable part of their trade was to serve the needs of inhabited islands in the Firth of Clyde. Some worked through to the east coast along the narrow waters of the Forth and Clyde Canal; these boats were limited to dimensions of 66 feet long, 18 feet beam and 8 feet deep.

It is said that the general design of the puffer helped to inspire the modern oil tanker, having engine and wheelhouse well towards the stern and appearing lower in the water at this end. They had much in common with Weaver flats (steam flats), but with greater freeboard and higher superstructure. There was a small foredeck with winches and a single mast with derrick or jib crane, the mast fitting into a tabernacle. Under the deck were forecastle quarters known as the *den*. This was occupied by the crew of two or three men and a boy. Between the den and the engine room was a deep oblong hold able to take 120 tons of cargo. The wheelhouse was just behind the tall funnel and often fairly high but uncovered. Later types were covered in but early puffers were steered even further back, at deck level, in the open.

The boiler had the minimum number of tubes working to a pressure of 120 pounds per square inch. In the absence of a fan there was a collar on top of the funnel known as a *lum hat* or *chimney hat*. Engines were two-cylinder compounds. The early types exhausted steam directly up the funnel into the atmosphere,

Fig. 30. Puffer.

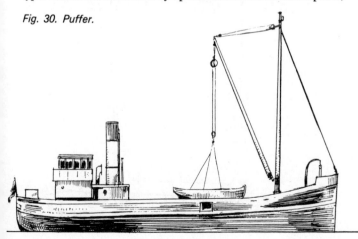

making the characteristic puffing noise. This was later improved by the addition of a condenser, which cut out the 'puff', although not before the name was widely accepted.

Appearing at the Clyde ports for about ninety years, they were immortalised in the tales of Neil Monro with his adventures of Para Handy in the fictional puffer the *Vital Spark*. The first vessels of this type were mainly restricted to the firth or estuary of the Clyde and the Forth and Clyde Canal. The first sea-going puffer was the *Cyclops,* a stern wheeler built in 1831. This was 68 feet long, with a beam of 15 feet 6 inches and about 7 feet 3 inches deep from keel to deck; weight including engine and boiler was about 38 tons.

13. Mersey and Weaver flats

Mersey flats were not widely used until the improvement of the Mersey Navigation during the first half of the eighteenth century. They also plied on the rivers Irwell and Weaver, especially the

Fig. 31. Mersey flat.

latter, and are sometimes known as Weaver flats, although many regard these as a distinctive type.

The original Mersey flat, which changed very little from the 1730s to the 1890s, was a double-ended barge with rounded bilges and carvel build. Stem and stern post were more or less raked, although the stern was sometimes more raked than the bow. There were usually, but not always, two masts. The fore mast, stepped a quarter of the way down the length of the craft — measured from the stem post — fitted into a tabernacle. A mizzen mast was stepped on the stern deck at the rear of the cargo space.

The flat, unlike most river craft of its type, was fully decked with hatches before and behind the fore mast. There was a living cabin or cuddy in the stern, usually occupied by a two-man crew or master and mate. The large elegant rudder was steered by means of a long, slightly curved tiller, not unlike the steerage of a canal boat but on a larger scale. Flats seldom carried leeboards.

The average Mersey flat was strongly built; the main timbers were of English oak with bilge planks of rock elm and planking (for midships) of oak or pitch pine. The flat was between 62 and 70 feet long, 6 feet deep and with a beam of 14 feet 9 inches to 17 feet. They could load up to 80 tons of cargo. A few early types on the Weaver appear to have been square and flat at the stern end. In later years some of the former sailing flats were turned into dumb barges for horse haulage or towing by tugs.

The Weaver steam flat

A number of these were used on the river Weaver from the late 1880s, especially in the salt and chemical industries. They were originally built of wood and steered from deck level. Later types were all-steel and had a raised wheelhouse. Length was 90 feet and beam 21 feet, with a capacity of 250 tons. They were still at work on the Weaver and Mersey until the early 1960s.

14. Short boats

These were canal boats, broad yet squat, designed to fit the short but wide beam locks of the Leeds and Liverpool Canal. Certain of the Leeds and Liverpool locks were 10 feet shorter than those on the majority of canals, especially the narrow waterways of the Midlands. The short boat was originally of wooden construction, horse-drawn or bow-hauled from the towing path. Its length was 62 feet, beam 14 feet 3 inches, and draught 3 feet 9 inches fully loaded. Cargo capacity was 50 tons. A stern cabin was constructed below deck level, while many—but not all—also had a fore cabin. Horse towing was gradually but not entirely replaced by steam power during the 1880s, although many former horse boats

Fig. 32. Horse-drawn short boat.

continued to be hauled by steam tugs and were otherwise known as **dumb barges.**

The design of the craft was thoroughly workmanlike with bluff bows and transom stern. Both stem and stern were frequently decorated with scrollwork and ornamental lettering in a strangely nautical style, quite different from the homely roses and castles of the narrowboats seen further south.

Although limited horse towing remained until the mid 1950s, the early steamers were popular as they could work longer shifts, both day and night. The first steamers were merely adapted from horse boats but later ones were purpose-built. Living quarters on the new type were confined to the fore cabin, while the space in the stern was occupied by engine and boiler. The steam boats usually worked in pairs, drawing a dumb barge or former horse boat. Both horse boats and steamers were family boats. There were steamers on the Leeds and Liverpool Canal at least until the late 1950s; the last of this type was constructed shortly before the Second World War. They mainly had wooden hulls until the 1920s, when they were replaced by steel-hulled craft.

Fig. 33. Powered short boat.

During the late 1920s diesel power began to supplement if not to replace steam. The smaller engine-room space of the diesel craft and the reduced amount of fuel space enabled new boats to carry an extra 15 tons of cargo. A number of all-steel diesel-powered short boats were constructed for British Waterways during the early 1950s, although most of this traffic ceased by 1970. The last short boat in regular commercial use traded over the Leigh branch of the Leeds and Liverpool Canal up to 1972. The few remaining types are either maintenance craft or preserved by amateur boaters for leisure purposes.

15. Severn trows

This type of craft, now extinct, operated mainly in the Severn estuary, although many worked as far inland as Stourport, Bewdley, Shrewsbury and the Welsh Marches. There were both large and small types, of clinker build, the larger having a length of 70 feet and beam of 17 feet. When empty they drew between 3 and 4 feet; they would carry about 120 tons on a draught of from 8 feet 6 inches to 9 feet 6 inches. Most of the larger types were confined to the Severn, Bristol Channel and the Avon to Bristol. Smaller vessels, of much the same type, found their way on to the Stroudwater Navigation via the Gloucester and Sharpness Canal and on to the Droitwich Canal. The latter, known as **Wich barges,** were mainly engaged in the salt trade.

The earliest ancestors of the Severn trow were using the Severn waterway (at one time the busiest waterway in England) from Anglo-Saxon times, although at this period and during the middle ages they were double-ended and resembled keels. By the seventeenth century they had acquired a distinctive D-shaped transom, sometimes sloping slightly inwards. The original mast was stepped slightly forward of the centre or midships and carried a large square sail. During the early part of the nineteenth century a mizzen mast began to appear, sometimes with a triangular or lateen sail having the mast in the centre, but more frequently with a standing gaff or spar. Most types were converted to fore and aft rig during the 1850s.

There was usually a crew of three, accommodated in forecastle quarters under the tiny fore deck. The captain had a cabin aft, under the stern deck. Space between was the cargo hold, open to the sky and rarely covered by hatches, there being no side decks. The mast was supported by crosswise or thwartship beams. There were fairly high bulwarks protecting stem and stern. When venturing far out into the Bristol Channel, or in rough weather, protective side cloths on rails and stanchions helped to shield the cargo.

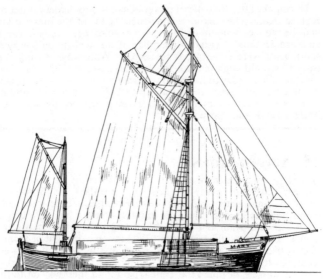

Fig. 34. Severn trow, box type.

The genuine trow was flat-bottomed with no external keel but had rounded bilges rather than chine build. Leeboards were not used but many trows had a removable false keel, necessary when sailing to windward. This was lowered over the side by means of chains and floated into position as need arose.

As the number of trows gradually declined on inland waters, a few were converted for work almost exclusively in the Bristol Channel, reaching the ports of South Wales and numerous harbours and inlets along the Devon coast. For this purpose covered hatches were fitted and bulwarks constructed from stem to stern, changing what was known as the **open mould type** to the later **box trow.**

Iron and steel hulls were introduced during the middle and late nineteenth century; the first trow with an iron hull was built for Danks and Sons of Stourport in 1843. Wooden hulls, however, were constructed until the twentieth century and noted for their strength and longevity. The wooden-hulled *William,* built in 1809, was still in service until 1939 when she was wrecked and ceased to be the oldest trading vessel in or around the British Isles.

Many trows ended their days either fitted with diesel engines or as dumb barges, without rigging, hauled by tugs and other vessels.

The author recollects seeing a dismasted trow in the Diglis Basin, Worcester, during the 1950s, although few survived the Second World War. Severn trows frequently used the barge basin at Stourport until the First World War. In the main street of that town there is a public house named the Severn Trow which has a fine scale model of the craft as an inn sign.

16. Severn tankers

These plied on the Severn between the estuary ports and the storage depots of the west Midlands, mainly at Stourport, Worcester and Gloucester. They were all-steel barges, powered by diesel engines and limited to a length of 137 feet to Worcester, with a beam of 22 feet and draught of 8 feet. Those working above Worcester to Stourport were less than 89 feet in length, 18 feet 11 inches in beam and 5 feet 9 inches in draught. The average length of craft between Worcester and Gloucester tended to be 100 feet with a beam of 8 feet, loading to a capacity of 500 tons. The normal cargo was fuel oil, running a frequent service from 1928 until the mid 1960s. The barges were eventually replaced by pipelines and improved road and rail delivery services, using bulk tankers.

17. Avon tar barges

These were part of a small fleet working over the Avon section of the Kennet and Avon Navigation. They worked under sail until the period of the First World War but were later converted to diesel power. The service began during the late 1860s and ended in 1967, finally replaced by road tankers able to operate into Wales via the new Severn Road Bridge. Although mainly confined to the river Avon a number worked across the Bristol Channel to the ports of South Wales, especially Cardiff and Newport. The Avon tar barge was bluff in the bows with a rounded counter stern. There was a tall wheelhouse and a short mast directly behind the cargo space. The bows had a raised fore deck mounting a large windlass.

18. Stroudwater barges

These craft were used on the Stroudwater Canal, also working into the Gloucester and Sharpness Canal, via Saul Junction. The Stroudwater Canal has been dewatered for many years, apart from a short section used for mooring at the Saul end. The last boats of this type, mainly towed from the bank, changed very little during a hundred years or more. They were about 70 feet long, with a beam of 15 feet 6 inches, and between 70 and 75 tons in capacity. They were fairly high at the stem post with bluff bows and rounded bilges. Like most barges on the English waterways they were of carvel build. There was a small decked area at both stem and stern with a large windlass mounted on the bows and a living cabin under the stern deck. Stroudwater barges were last used during the 1940s, some being retained on the Gloucester and Sharpness Canal as dumb barges.

19. Teignmouth keels

A sailing keel of the South-west, about 56 feet long with a 13 foot 6 inch beam, loading to upwards of 30 tons, this type of craft was mainly used on the river Teign in South Devon and on the short canals of Devon and Cornwall, connecting with quarries and open-cast workings for china clay. They were rigged with a square sail on a single mast but were also frequently towed from the bank. Many were made redundant towards the end of the nineteenth century by improved railway services. Later types were often smaller, about 50 feet long, although some may have been broader in the beam than the average type. Depth for most craft was about 5 feet. They had rounded bows and flat, transom sterns. There were sixteen still in service until 1931 but mainly dismasted and towed in trains by diesel tugs.

Fig. 35. Teignmouth keel.

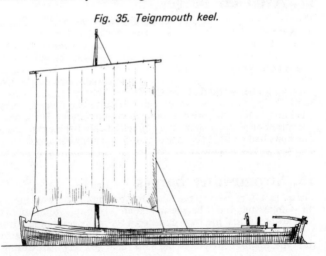

20. Narrowboats

These were used on the narrow canals and limited by the gauge of the locks and bridgeholes to dimensions of less than 70 feet by 7 feet 2 inches. They travelled to nearly all parts of the inland waterways, on both canals and rivers. Their length prohibited full navigation of the Leeds and Liverpool Canal but they could otherwise travel from the industrial heart of England to Mersey, Humber, Thames and Severn, even penetrating a short distance into North Wales along the Welsh section of the Shropshire Union Canal. At times they were seen on the tidal reaches of the Thames, either breasted up (several side by side) or rigged with a temporary or jury mast and square sail. They were not, however, suitable for passage over broad rivers and estuaries in any but the calmest weather.

The earliest type of canal craft in England may have been the cigar-shaped **starvationer** worked in flooded galleries of the Duke of Bridgewater's coal mines at Worsley near Manchester. They worked several miles underground, using inclined planes for changes of level, and were operated by men wearing special harness, which could be hooked to rings projecting from the tunnel walls, and walking the boat as though on a treadmill. In other parts the boats could be legged by kicking against the roof or side walls with metal-shod boots. These boats were of oval shape and double-ended, about 20 feet long.

The Bridgewater Canal, from the mines at Worsley to the centre of Manchester and later to a junction with the river Mersey at Runcorn, was one of the first important canal navigations in the country, constructed by the Duke of Bridgewater with James Brindley as his chief engineer and adviser. It was mainly to supply Manchester with cheap coal, undercutting both packhorse trains and river navigations. In the course of time there were boats both for merchandise and for passenger traffic, the latter known as **packet boats.** One of the passenger types, the Duchess-Countess, survived well into the twentieth century, and it is obvious from her design that such craft were the prototypes of narrowboats used on the inland waterways for over two hundred years. The man usually credited with the design of commercial narrowboats was Thomas Monk of Tipton, in the Black Country, after whom they were nicknamed 'monkey boats'. In the West of England and on the Severn (at one time large numbers of narrowboats could be seen on this navigation between Bewdley and Gloucester) they were known as **long boats.**

In the early days the narrowboats were mainly horse-drawn, working either in pairs or as singles, sometimes with two horses or mules or a pair of donkeys in tandem. The general rule, however, was a single boat and horse. While mules were hardier than horses and cheaper to feed, for much the same amount of work, they frequently lacked the willingness or obedience of horses and were less reliable than the average horse. Donkeys, known as 'animals', were useful on some navigations, being small enough to climb into the boat on reaching tunnels without towing paths.

Steam-powered canal boats or **steamers** began to appear during the second half of the nineteeth century, but there were still plenty of horse boats until after the First World War, when they were gradually superseded, except on short or branch canals, by motorboats with internal-combustion engines. There were still one or two horse boats on the Birmingham Canal Navigations as late as the 1970s.

Family boats

From the late eighteenth to the mid nineteenth centuries narrowboats were usually worked by one or two men to each boat. Some slept on the boats in the stern cabins but many worked a system of stages, changing boats in opposite directions and spending the nights in canalside inns or hostels, where there were also stables for the horses.

During the 1840s and 1850s there was a period of keen competition with the railway companies and as a result the boater was forced to leave his cottage on the land, to which he might return like a sailor on leave, and take his family into the boat. This was a double economy as wife and children helped to crew the boat, while saving the rent of other accommodation. Although there may have been a few family boats before the 1840s, from this period onwards family boats began to increase in numbers and the few remaining craft worked by men only were **fly boats,** often working round the clock with perishable cargoes. The standard living cabin was about 10 feet long and 6 feet 6 inches wide, entered through double doors or hatches from a small stern deck. The boat was steered from a footboard or step in the doorway. At

Fig. 36. Canal narrowboats: motorboat (top) and butty.

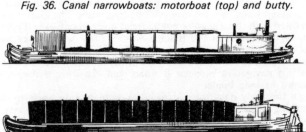

Fig. 37. 'Joshers' breasted up (side by side).

night the tiller would be reversed, the double doors closed and a slide drawn over the top or well of the cockpit. On the left of the cabin entrance was a heating and cooking stove, sometimes raised above deck level on a low platform, surrounded by gleaming pots and pans. The stovepipe or chimney disappeared through a hole in the roof, bound at the top with brass rings or rims. Opposite the stove was a lengthwise bench that could be turned into a bed or bunk at night for use by a child. Other children might sleep in a small fore cabin. A crossbed let down from the side wall, at the upper end of the cabin; this part was divided from the living quarters at night by lace curtains and was known as the *bedroom*. What was termed the *table-cupboard* fitted into an angle between bed and stove, the table letting down from the front of a crock cupboard with drawers and cupboards underneath. The interiors of most boat cabins were grained and varnished, with ornamental panels displaying the traditional roses and castles. There were also lace and crochetwork hangings and lace plates or brass ornaments filling every possible corner. The crock cupboard would have a display of Staffordshire china figures and the celebrated Measham ware, used mainly for teapots, milk jugs and water jugs.

Working pairs

From the 1920s many of the canal families changed from horse boats to diesel power, which was cheaper and almost trouble-free. The first diesel-powered boats, fitted with Swedish Bolinder two-stroke engines, were often converted horse boats made of wood, with elm bottoms and oak frameworks, daubed with a protective layer of 'chalico' (a mixture of horse dung, cow-hair and hot tar). Eventually all-steel boats or composite boats were introduced, the latter having steel sides and elm bottoms.

The old wooden boat was retained as a dumb boat or **butty** towed behind the motorboat. Together these were known as a working pair or **joshers,** this being boater's slang (of Black Country origin) for old pals or comrades. With a large family, the children slept in the cabin of the motorboat. Interiors of the stern cabins on both horse boats and motorboats were very similar but the motorboat cabin often had a door opening into the engine room or 'hole', also approached from double side doors. The stern deck of the motorboat had a flat counter or rounded shape, while the tiller was a metal bar of Z shape, painted with stripes not unlike a barber's pole. The tiller on the butty or horse boat was curved or bow-shaped and fitted into a tall, backward-sloping rudder post or ram's head ornamented with cords and knots, scrubbed to snowy whiteness and known as the *Turk's head* and *swan's neck*. Most family boats were kept in spotless condition, apart from a few known as **Rodney boats** or floating slums, usually in the hands of people new to the waterways, shunned by the long-established and often clannish canal families of tradition.

From the 1930s motorboats were usually fitted with four-stroke twin engines of a type they retained until the present day. The modern engine room between cabin and cargo space was reached

Fig. 38. Prow of a narrowboat: 1 top planks; 2 mast; 3 stand; 4 strut; 5 running block; 6 catch; 7 lamp; 8 deck lid.

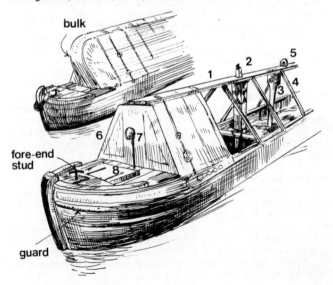

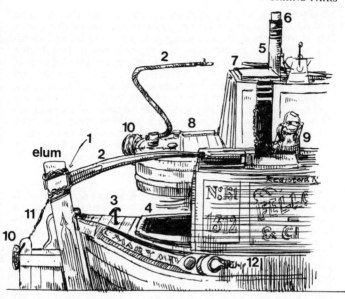

Fig. 39. Stern ends of narrowboats: 1 Turk's head; 2 tillers; 3 stud; 4 cockpit; 5 stove chimney; 6 chimney can; 7 slide or hatch cover; 8 counter stern; 9 water can; 10 stern fenders; 11 swan's neck; 12 shackles.

along catwalks about six inches wide, on both sides of the boat. These are known as *gunnels,* being along the upper line or gunwales, and greatly reduce the inner width of the engine room, which is normally about 8 feet 6 inches long and 5 feet 9 inches beam.

Day boats

These were known in the Black Country as **Joey boats** and were mainly worked over the Birmingham Canal Navigations and adjacent waterways, usually on short day trips. Many were double-ended and able to transfer the rudder from one end to the other to avoid turning in a confined space, for there were few turning places or winding holes in this area. With the advent of steam and diesel tugs the towing posts changed position and were eventually abandoned, often moved nearer the ends and away from the quarters. Long strings of day boats were lashed together by the dozen, only the last boat having a rudder. Horse-drawn day boats

63

remained well into the twentieth century, especially the open rubbish boats used for factory waste in the Birmingham area. Horses were also used in assisting powered day boats and strings of unpowered boats drawn by tugs through various lock flights.

The day boat, although sometimes without any form of shelter, usually had a small cabin in the stern. This was smaller than the cabin of a family boat and furnished only with an L-shaped bench, a small locker or shelf and an upright bottle-stove. This was mainly a heating stove but had a bar or trivet in front of the firebox door on which a pot or kettle could be fixed. The main function was to provide a sheltered space in which to eat meals and brew hot drinks. Most cabins were 4 feet long by 6 feet wide but slightly narrower on the side nearest the double doors.

The Shroppie fly

This was a long narrowboat, round-bilged and streamlined. It was only 6 feet wide by 2 feet deep. They were used for urgent and perishable goods over the Shropshire Union Canal, between the Mersey ports and Birmingham or other Midland centres. They were made of wood and towed by two galloping horses, worked in tandem and relays, and able to travel at well over ten miles an hour. These boats worked round the clock in the charge of young, single men.

Runcorn boats

These massive canal boats owned by the Runcorn Company had barrel-shaped holds and near-vertical stem and stern posts (stern posts were usually raked on other craft). They operated on the Bridgewater and Shropshire Union Canals and were more like barges than ordinary narrowboats. They were converted to motorboats about 1914, just before the First World War. Some worked into the Midlands and two of the 'converted' type, having a propeller shaft through the stern post with false cheeks or side pieces (forming a counter stern), are preserved on the Birmingham Canal Navigations.

Ampton boats

These were unusual craft 80 feet long, much longer than the normal canal craft as they worked exclusively over a stretch of water without locks, between collieries on Cannock Chase and the Wolverhampton area.

FMC boats

These were narrowboats owned by the haulage firm of Fellows Morton and Clayton; they were sometimes known as **Joshers** after Joshua Clayton, one of the founders of the firm. They were light, fast boats, seldom used for dirty cargoes such as coal or coke. They often worked 'fly' or night-time services with perishable goods. In design they were well raked at stem and stern, being fairly low in the water. The tumblehome of the cabin sides sloped inwards more than on other boats. FMC boats might be termed the aristocrats of the narrow waterways.

Barlow boats

These operated in the coal trade, mainly from Birmingham. The stern cabins were usually flush-sided without the usual square or oblong panels with which many narrowboats were decorated. The front board or triangular cratch was noted for its colourful decorations but was more upright than on FMC boats and other types. Masts and stands above the cargo space, supporting the tent-like side cloths and waterproof covers, were much higher than on other boats, while there were planks or washboards (at the end near the stern cabin) to prevent small coal or coke from slipping into the water.

Ricky boats

These were built by Messrs Walkers Limited of Rickmansworth for use on the Grand Union Canal. They were wooden craft, worked mainly south of Birmingham and had higher sides and stands than the average narrowboats of the Midlands. The cabin sides were also fairly high and straight but with deeply recessed side panels. Being high-sided they were easier than most narrow craft to navigate on broad rivers and estuaries, frequently working over tidal reaches of the Thames below Brentford.

Grand Union Canal boats

The Grand Union Canal Company was a great carrier on its own line between the two world wars. It pioneered the use of steel and composite boats to replace former wooden boats. Like the earlier Ricky boats, they had plenty of freeboard that kept out waves and wash on tidal reaches.

Boats of the GUCC fleet of the 1930s, launched to coincide with a programme of widening, dredging and modernisation on the line of the canal, between London and Birmingham, were of extra depth and stronger construction than most other boats of the period. They were divided into various classes, the smallest being the 'Star' class, all named after stars or heavenly bodies. This type was slightly larger than the FMC boats. The 'Town' class was much larger, with a hold about 5 feet deep and having considerable freeboard. It was specially designed for loading and unloading from sea-going ships either in the Thames or in the London docks. The largest of all were the 'Royalty' class, named after kings and queens, of which only six were constructed. These were slightly larger than 'Town' class boats but even sturdier. One

GRAND UNION CANAL BOATS

of the few survivors, originally *Victoria* but renamed *Linda*, was preserved by an enthusiast on the Birmingham Canal Navigations.

Gas boats

A number of converted narrowboats were used to convey bulk liquids on the canals. The largest number operated for Thomas Clayton of Oldbury for about eighty years until 1966, mainly carrying cargoes of gas-water, oil and tar. The tank space was decked over with double layers of planking and the fillers were sealed before each trip. Interior swillboards broke the free flow of liquids. Many were family boats with large stern and fore cabins, although the fore cabin was also a storage space for extra fenders. Day boats, on shorter hauls, were all black but the family boats had painted cabins. There were both horse and powered boats. One of the last horse boats, restored in 1971, is now owned by the Boat Museum at Ellesmere Port. This was the *Gifford*, sold to a private trader in 1966 and mule-hauled for several trips. Fodder for the horse or mule was kept under a form of cratch near the fore end.

'River' class boats

These were designed for and used by the British Waterways Authority in 1958. They were butties or unpowered boats, normally towed by 'Admiral' class tugs, designed about the same period. Sometimes known as **blue tops** because of their unusual blue covers of fibreglass, which replaced the traditional side cloths and tarpaulins of earlier craft, they were blunt- or bluff-ended and made from sheets of welded light-gauge steel. Intended to be a revolutionary type of craft, they may have arrived too late to make the desired impression and were far from popular with the few remaining but conservative boaters of the 1960s.

21. Steam narrowboats

These were used mainly on the Grand Junction Canal during the second half of the nineteenth century. The first types were wooden boats used from the 1860s by the Grand Junction Canal Company and eventually sold to Fellows Morton and Clayton. In 1910 FMC built a fleet of steel-hulled steamers for their own use. Despite efforts to keep them in spotless condition, including anti-dust curtains and floor coverings, they were difficult to maintain to the general high standards of the FMC fleet. A great deal of cargo space was taken up by the engine, boiler and supply of solid fuel, while extra crewmen were needed to stoke the fires and look after the engines. These were great disadvantages and by the 1920s most of the steam boats on the Grand Junction Canal had been replaced

Fig. 40. Steam narrowboat.

by craft with internal-combustion engines. Many of the original steamers were later fitted with internal-combustion engines, which made extra cargo space available.

The cargo space of a steam narrowboat was only 39 feet in length — for steering and general handling purposes — which was more than 12 feet less than a horse-drawn narrowboat.

22. Welsh narrowboats

These craft operated over the mainly industrial canals and waterways of South Wales, especially in the Swansea Valley and Taff Vale. They were often shorter but much wider than English narrowboats or those using the Welsh section of the Shropshire Union Canal in North Wales. The canals of South Wales were separate lines not connected with any other part of the system, nor generally with each other.

They were all day boats, in some ways similar to the Joey boats of the Birmingham Canal Navigations. They were mainly double-ended, the rudder being transferred from one end to the other to save turning. Some were without any form of shelter, although the majority had a small cabin for the preparation and eating of meals. The bows of the Welsh boats were almost vertical and in some cases curved slightly forwards and outwards, the opposite of the raked bows on English narrowboats. A double row of heavy strakes or guards often ran down the entire length of each side. The boats were 60 to 65 feet long, with a beam of between 7 feet 6 inches and 9 feet, depending on the size of locks on each waterway. While the Kennet and Avon Canal was operated by the Great Western Railway Company (during the 1920s), several Welsh boats were transferred to this navigation for use in maintenance work.

23. Tub boats

Tub boats, apart from the almost square-shaped Tom puddings of the Aire and Calder Navigations, were used on a number of specially designed canals in all parts of Britain, ranging from the Midlands to Wales and the South-west, especially Cornwall. They were rectangular floating boxes towed in trains, usually from the bank. On some canals in South Wales they were bow-hauled by men and women or youths and girls, but in most cases they were drawn by a single horse. Although most were square-ended, on some canals the first boat would have ordinary or pointed bows. On the Torrington Canal in North Devon boats were in pairs, close-coupled, the first boat having pointed bows while the second boat was square-ended.

On most tub-boat canals either inclined planes or lifts were used in place of locks. Where there was a change of level the boats would be drawn up a specially designed slipway or even a narrow-gauge railway. On some canals, such as the Bude Canal in Cornwall, the boats even had fixed wheels, while on the Grand Western Canal they were designed to fit into the compartments of special lifts.

24. Packet boats

These were passenger boats appearing on the inland waterways almost from the time of their inception. They offered a regular service between waterside towns and villages that may well have been swifter, safer and more comfortable than travelling over badly made roads in lumbering stage-wagons.

The swiftest and most efficient packet boats were drawn by teams of cantering or galloping horses ridden by postilions and changed at various intervals along the towing paths. They were fly boats or priority traffic, given right of way on all parts of the navigation, especially at locks and bridgeholes. On the

Fig. 41. Horse-drawn packet boat, small type.

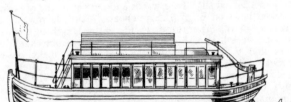

Fig. 42. The 'Lord Dundas'.

Bridgewater Canal some horse-drawn packet boats had a curved blade fitted at the fore end to cut through the towing ropes of other craft unable or unwilling to let the packet boat overtake.

Many packet boats had facilities for eating and sleeping, with coffee-house refreshments at all hours of the day. Packets between Bradford-on-Avon and Bath even boasted light entertainment and a string band.

In some areas packet boats continued long after the challenge of railways, although with the accent more on viewing local scenery than on taking the quickest or shortest route. Many were eventually powered by steam and travelled on both canals and rivers. At one time there were regular steam-packet services between Leeds and Goole and between Lincoln and Boston. On the Gloucester and Sharpness Canal steam packet boats continued until well into the twentieth century, providing something akin to a country bus service in an area isolated from both main roads and railways, except at either end of the canal.

An early packet boat, the *Lord Dundas,* constructed by Messrs Fairbairn and Lillie of Manchester, operated on the Forth and Clyde Canal from the early 1830s. In some ways it resembled the ill-fated tug *Charlotte Dundas,* banned from the same waterway for causing too much wash and eroding the banks. By the 1830s, however, there had been a reinvestigation into the hazards of excessive wash (although the subject appears to have been reconsidered at later times) and the Forth and Clyde directors were prepared on this occasion to take a risk. Like the *Charlotte Dundas* the *Lord Dundas* had a paddle-wheel in the centre of the deck and, until the introduction of driving screws, centre and stern paddles were preferred to side paddles, especially on narrow and still-water navigations. The 10 foot paddle of the *Lord Dundas* was driven by a 10-horsepower engine, almost amidships. There were two passenger saloons or compartments, able to carry 150 passengers.

Packet and passenger boats on the Regent's Canal in London were widely used throughout the nineteenth century; they have a parallel in the modern Thames water bus and the canal bus service running to the zoo in Regent's Park, through which the Regent's Canal passes.

25. Tugs

The use of tugs on canals and inland waterways has long been a matter of heated controversy. While having several clear advantages over the use of men or animals for towing, tugs were often criticised for causing bank erosion and silting through the wash from their paddles or screws. Numerous experiments were carried out in several countries during the late eighteenth and early nineteenth centuries, many of these being for steam tugs to assist large sailing vessels in harbours and estuaries. The first successful attempt to harness steam power to canal traffic was by means of a tug with a centre-stern paddle, the *Charlotte Dundas,* constructed by an inventor named Symington for the Forth and Clyde Canal. This towed a pair of dumb barges, loaded with 70 tons of cargo each, a distance of 19 miles at an average speed of 2½ miles per hour. The *Charlotte Dundas,* however, was condemned for causing too much wash and never used in regular service, although eight similar tugs were ordered by (but not supplied to) the Duke of Bridgewater for use on the waterways between Worsley and Runcorn. The experiment took place in 1801 but the Duke died two years later and his instructions were not carried out. Steam tugs were at first greatly disliked by other boaters and the first tug on the Bridgewater Canal, the *Bonapart,* was withdrawn after a short period for throwing too much water on to banks and towing paths.

With the coming of the railways canal authorities began to re-examine the use of tugs, trying to regain their lost traffic through greater speed and more efficient handling. This, however, was something of a forlorn hope, especially as the railways began to buy up the canals and tried to convert as many public users as possible from waterways to the new iron roads. In this connection one is reminded of the controversy caused by the use of Inshaw's screw-driven steam tug *Pioneer* on the Ashby Canal (the Moira cut), then owned by the Midland Railway Company, which led to a celebrated lawsuit of the 1850s, restricting the speed of the boat to a level at which it became far less economical.

Fig. 43. Steam tug.

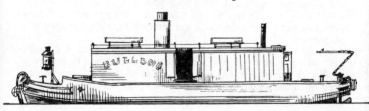

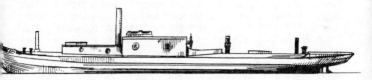

Fig. 44. The tug 'Sharpness'.

Steam tugs, however, enjoyed a revival towards the end of the nineteenth century; they were of particular use in tunnels without towing paths, where much time and energy were formerly wasted by legging or shafting a boat through while the horse was led over the top. Tugs were mainly used for short hauls on canals connected with dockland areas, where there might be obstructions along the wharves and towing paths. The Bridgewater Canal system, taken over by the Bridgewater Navigation Company Limited in 1872 from the trustees of the Duke of Bridgewater, soon began to employ steam towage on an extensive scale. They began by ordering twenty-six small tugs of a type that was familiar in the area for about seventy-five years. These were known locally as the **little packets.** They were based on a packet dock near the top locks at Runcorn, where they were bunkered and serviced. Their main work was to draw flats and unpowered canal boats between Runcorn and Manchester, which took about eight hours with a full load. A number of the surviving tugs were converted to diesel power during the 1920s.

Steam tugs were also widely used on the Gloucester and Sharpness Canal, especially between Sharpness and Gloucester docks. Unlike horses, limited to one or two barges, they could draw whole trains of fully loaded craft, working all round the clock. At Gloucester cargoes were transferred to long boats (narrowboats) and towed upstream in trains to several inland ports. The steam tugs on this line were converted to diesel power after the Second World War.

In the London area steam-powered tugs were used on the Regent's Canal, working through to Limehouse docks, from 1855. On longer navigations radiating from London self-powered steam boats were preferred, as these took up less space in the numerous locks. Steam tugs for tunnels were introduced in 1871 on the Grand Junction Canal, which became the Grand Union Canal in 1929, and remained until 1934.

During the second decade of the twentieth century the internal-combustion engine began to challenge the steamer, first for tugs but later for all forms of power-driven boat and barge. One of the first notable internal-combustion-engined tugs was the *Sharpness*, built in 1908 by Messrs Abdela and Mitchell Limited and based on the

Severn and Thames Canal. Several others of similar type, working on the Worcester and Birmingham Canal and the upper navigable reaches of the Severn, were also constructed about the same period. They all had steel hulls and were 45 feet long with a beam of just under 7 feet and draught of 4 feet. Their petrol or paraffin engines were 30 horsepower, turning a four-bladed screw. *Sharpness* was mainly used as a tunnel tug and soon transferred for duties on the Worcester and Birmingham Canal, based at Tardebigge and Shortwood, where she was also an icebreaker. She is now in private hands on the Lower Avon Navigation, used as a pleasure cruiser. Most power tugs had wheel rather than tiller steering, usually at deck level.

Steam and diesel tugs were and are used on the Aire and Calder Navigations to draw trains of compartment boats or Tom puddings. These were about 25 feet in length.

A tunnel tug in the Harecastle Tunnel (new line) of the Trent and Mersey Canal used electrical power for a number of years and was still operating by the mid 1940s. The prototype was run from batteries carried in a separate boat but was later converted to taking power from an overhead wire to which a pole or boom was raised, similar to the pole on a tram or trolley bus. Similar experiments were also made on the Staffordshire and Worcestershire Canal but were short-lived.

26. Dredgers

The most primitive type of dredger, widely used on the narrow canals, is the **spoon dredger.** This consists of large wooden or iron spoons mounted on a boat or flat and used for scooping mud from the bottom of a canal or waterway. The mud is deposited either on the bank or in the holds of special rubbish barges or mud hoppers for transport to a tipping site. Each dredger of this type is manned by a crew of three and a helmsman. One man guides the spoon and two work the crane or derrick to which it may be attached by chain and pulley.

In later years more sophisticated methods of dredging have been adopted, although these are often complex and expensive. They include the use of suction pipes, buckets and endless chains, on river navigations and in estuaries, and even a type of excavator mounted to work on a flat or raft. **Excavator dredgers** are sometimes seen on narrow canals, the floating platform from which they work having side flaps which can be raised for passing through locks.

The oldest steam dredger of the scoop type still in working order was designed by Isambard Kingdom Brunel, engineer of the Great Western Railway and other projects. It was constructed in 1844 and worked on the Bridgwater and Taunton Canal, mainly in Bridgwater docks. It is now restored and preserved, displayed at the Exeter Maritime Museum. Earlier steam dredgers were designed for work on the Thames and connected waterways by Richard Trevithick during the 1800s.

27. Icebreakers

There were two main types of icebreaker.. The earliest, used on both canals and rivers, was merely a tug or other craft with reinforced bows, forcing its way through the ice, as with larger sea-going icebreakers used in the Baltic. The other type, mainly used on canals and still-water navigations, was known as a **rocking boat;** it might be horse-drawn or powered by steam or diesel engines. There was a broad centre platform, with two uprights and a horizontal handrail, rope or bar to which a team of five or more men could cling, rocking backwards and forwards to clear the channel as the boat moved forward. Icebreakers were often towed by teams of heavy carthorses, hired from the railway companies. They were urged forward at the best speed they could muster and made an impressive sight, the icebreaker throwing up lumps of ice on to the banks with a loud cracking noise, to which would be added the thunder of hooves on the towing path.

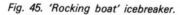

Fig. 45. 'Rocking boat' icebreaker.

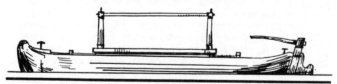

28. General-service boats and flats

Also known as **work flats,** these boats were used for maintenance on most inland navigations. A typical example usually had swim-ends or a swim-head and rounded or counter stern. It was usually a dumb boat or barge and seldom powered. The hold would be adapted to carry any type of equipment, tools or building materials, sometimes a load of clay puddle for mending weak places in the banks. Most had a small fore deck mounted with a windlass, also a large stern cabin with plenty of headroom. This was used as a lockup, shelter and office. Some work flats on the Grand Union Canal could be fitted with large brushes gauged to the walls and roof of a tunnel and used for cleaning away grit or soot that might otherwise fall into passing narrowboats.

29. Inspection boats and launches

These were used on both rivers and canals for the purpose of ordinary inspection, by the engineering staff of a particular navigation. Once a year, however, they were at the disposal of the directors of the company for an annual tour of inspection. Inspection boats were usually quite elaborate affairs, all teak and polished silver, with cut glass or finely etched windows. The annual inspection was often an excuse for feasting and celebrations on the grand scale. In the early days inspection craft were horse-drawn, the horses ridden by postilions in livery. Later types were either converted to steam power or purpose-built steamers. An inspection boat built for the Grand Union Canal Company during the late 1920s, however, had a petrol engine, but this was rare.

One of the better-known canal inspection boats was *The Lady Hatherton,* used by directors of the Staffordshire and Worcestershire Canal Company from the late 1890s until the 1930s. It had elaborate interior fittings but was later given a new, almost identical hull and converted into a pleasure yacht.

Several individuals had private inspection launches or state barges in which they could tour the inland waterways, although these were limited to a few rich and influential people, often with a vested interest in rivers and canals. They were not pleasure cruisers in the ordinary sense but may have been the precursors of pleasure-boat traffic. One of the early horse-drawn types, operated by the Earl of Ellesmere on the Bridgewater Canal, later acquired a small petrol engine, ending its days as a tripper boat in and around Manchester docks. Mr H. R. de Salis, the author of many reference books on the waterways and a director of Fellows Morton and Clayton Limited, had a specially built steam launch,

Fig. 46. Steam inspection launch.

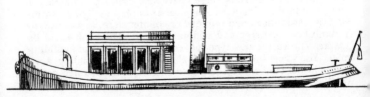

the *Dragonfly*, on which he toured the inland waterways of England. This was 59 feet long with a beam of 6 feet 8 inches and a draught of 2 feet 6 inches.

30. Pleasure steamers

Towards the end of the nineteenth century there was a great demand for both short trips and long excursions over the inland waterways, especially rivers. Many social factors were involved including a recognised need for annual holidays, the increased spending power of the lower and middle classes and an essentially civilised interest in what lay round the next bend in the road or river. There were also organised church or school trips and works outings on a scale previously unknown.

Special steamers were constructed for this need, partly covered over but with plenty of viewing space and seats facing both inwards and outwards, often at two or more levels. Such craft were either of clinker or carvel build and constructed to the dimensions of locks on the waterways over which they usually travelled. They were well raked fore and aft, often with a transom or counter stern, on the lines of a pleasure yacht. There were regular summer services on most navigable rivers, especially the Thames, Severn, Dee, Dart and Warwickshire Avon. Perhaps the most popular were run by Messrs Salter Brothers on the Thames, many starting from Oxford. Their first Oxford to Kingston service began during the 1880s. After the Second World War services on all waterways began to decline and the remaining steamers were replaced by more economical boats (for those days) with diesel engines.

Passenger services have also been provided in steamers and power-boats of considerable tonnage over the larger lochs or lakes of Britain and on the estuaries of Clyde, Thames and Severn. An outstanding example was the paddle steamer *Maid of the Loch* on Loch Lomond; it was 193 feet long with a 28 foot beam and a gross tonnage of 555 tons.

Fig. 47. Pleasure steamer for rivers, 1890s.

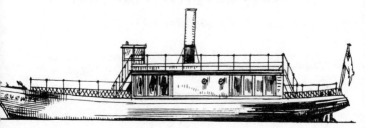

Fig. 48. Dart paddle steamer.

31. Cabin cruisers and converted narrowboats

Privately owned cabin cruisers have been widely used on the inland waterways since the early 1920s but were first confined to rivers, lakes and the Norfolk Broads, at least until after the Second World War. The decline of the waterways, especially the narrow canals, for commercial purposes has been paralleled by a whole spate of literature on the history, scenery and folklore of the canals. Perhaps the most popular and influential book was *Narrow Boat* by the late L. T. C. Rolt; it describes an interesting round trip on the canals of the Midlands and inspired many others to leave the more obvious rivers in search of different interests and scenery.

Many modern cruisers have hulls of reinforced plastic or fibreglass, in place of earlier wooden or steel hulls, and may be either of wide or narrow beam. The latter are also of shallow draught and specially designed for canal navigation. Both are fully fitted with bunks, cabin furniture, modern cookers, cupboard space, sanitation and television sets. One of the more popular types of wide-beam cruiser has a centre steering cockpit. Steering

Fig. 49. Cabin cruiser.

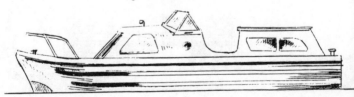

is usually by wheel rather than tiller. Dimensions vary according to type and cost, but the average broad-beam cruiser is about 28 feet by 9 feet 8 inches with 1 foot 10 inch draught. Narrow cruisers have to conform to narrowboat dimensions to pass the locks and bridgeholes of the narrow canals. Some craft have all-steel hulls and are more on the lines of traditional narrowboats, fitted with 8 horsepower internal-combustion engines. Narrow-beam cruisers frequently have outboard motors.

In recent years many former commercial boats and barges have been converted for use as cruisers and hotel boats. They are ideal for a large party or outing but tend to be too large for the needs of individuals or the average family group. Some yards, however, are still building narrowboats, for cruising purposes, to original designs and dimensions.

32. Ferries

Ferries were used across rivers and estuaries, usually where there were no bridges, to avoid considerable detours. Where rivers are very wide and navigated by large sea-going ships making their way to inland docks it is often costly to build bridges with high enough clearance, so that ferries may be termed floating bridges for both passengers and vehicles.

The earliest craft used for ferrying were dugouts and flat-bottomed punts, sometimes known as **pontoons** or **scows.** These were later supplemented by the more elegant skiff and wherry for passengers. The large square-ended type is still used for vehicles in certain areas, attached to landing stages on either side of the waterway by ropes or chains. Some ferries, with pointed stem and stern, drift across, the helmsman taking advantage of tide or current. Others are wound over by hand, especially smaller types on narrow rivers, the ferryman operating a windlass in the centre

Fig. 50. River Dart ferry.

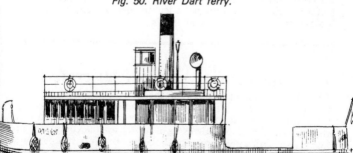

of the boat. This type included a number of so called horse ferries, widely used on the river Yare in Norfolk, to ferry horse traffic. Smaller passenger ferries could be hauled across by the operator pulling on a rope, about shoulder level, hand over hand. Chain ferries, a typical example of which crosses the river Medina at East Cowes, Isle of Wight, were guided by double chains on the bed of the river wound through drums on either side of the craft. These were originally steam-powered but later converted to diesel power.

On broad rivers or estuaries, such as the Mersey at Liverpool, the Thames at Gravesend and the Dart at Kingswear, there were quite large steamers, some of which still function, although the majority are now powered by diesel rather than steam. Many were capable of sea-going voyages and the *Mew* of the Dartmouth-Kingswear service was used in the Dunkirk rescue operations of 1940.

Other outstanding craft in this category are the Woolwich free ferries, able to take vehicles on the upper decks and passengers in a lower saloon. The present ferries are three in number, each carrying up to one thousand passengers and two hundred vehicles on a five-minute crossing. They replace four earlier steamers, with tall funnels placed at either end of the vehicle deck.

Three large ferry boats used to ply across the Humber between Hull and New Holland carrying the traffic that now uses the Humber Bridge, opened in 1981. One of them was the *Lincoln Castle,* a rare coal-fired paddle steamer. In the summer it was sometimes chartered for up-river cruises to Goole Docks and other places of interest. The Humber ferries were controlled by British Rail.

Three ferries formerly worked a passenger and vehicle service across the Severn between Aust and Beachley, until replaced by the Severn Road Bridge. The largest of these was *Severn King,* double-ended and fitted with a deck turntable that could take up to eighteen cars. The crossing of the Severn at this point was highly dangerous owing to fogs, tides and the Severn bores or miniature tidal waves. Services were frequently suspended and motor vehicles forced to make a lengthy detour or travel through the Severn Tunnel on special trains.

---

33. Contemporary commercial craft

While the commercial traffic of the narrow canals has greatly declined, some of the rivers and broad canals are still flourishing. There are healthy signs of revival, especially in the North-east, where two leading barge firms have revitalised the compartment-boat system with a new type of craft serving the Ferrybridge power station. These are huge oblong vessels of 210 tons capacity, coupled together like Tom puddings but pushed instead of pulled by a square-ended power-boat. They work in threes and are capable of delivering 1,000 tons of coal an hour to the power-station wharf, where they are run into a tippler and lifted 40 feet clear of the water; their loads are then fed into hoppers from an inverted position.

There are also interesting experiments with compartment boats from overseas, contained within a larger double-hulled vessel. The smaller craft are detached on reaching their home port, to be taken further inland by tugs. The most outstanding of these are the **Bacat** and **Lash** systems. The Bacat system works mainly across the North Sea with units capable of conveying 140 tons of freight, while the Lash system is used for Atlantic crossings. The host ship contains up to eighty-nine lighters, each lighter holding 435 tons of cargo. The lighters are lifted in and out of the host ship by means of a travelling overhead crane, operating from bridge to stern.

On certain narrow canals in the Potteries area special boats have been designed to operate for short runs with container loads of delicate china. Each carries about 20 tons of china.

Some owners of narrowboats are now converting their craft for pleasure trips in the summer but using them to carry household coal, which they often sell by the bag at the wharfside, in winter.

Fig. 51. Pusher tug.

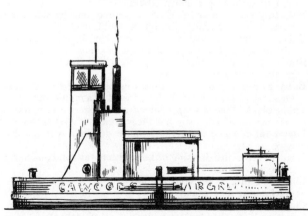

Glossary

Abaft: Towards the stern of a vessel.
Above board: Above deck level.
Aft: Behind or towards the stern.
After part: The rear or stern of a craft.
Amidships: The centre or middle part of a craft.
Astern: Behind. Usually at the rear of a vessel, as with a following craft.
Awash: (1) Washed over by waves or lying low, near the surface of the water. (2) The anchor of a craft is awash when lifted clear of the water.
Back door: Communicating door of a narrowboat, between cabin and hold or cargo space.
Barge: Large commercial craft used for conveying goods or minerals over the inland waterways. More than 7 foot beam. Also a small passenger or pleasure craft.
Bargee: Crewman or owner-skipper of a barge.
Boat: Any type of small craft on the inland waterways. Normally less than 7 foot beam.
Boater: Person living or working on a canal boat.
Bow hauliers: Men working in gangs to pull boats or barges, from the towing paths.
Box mast: Square-shaped box-like mast or upright of a canal boat. Often telescoping in two sections. Used as a towing post and to support protective covers.
Breasting up: Two or more boats secured side by side for river navigation or passing through a double lock.
Bulk: Ornamental structure of wood and light canvas, stuffed with hay, fitted to the front board or cratch of a narrowboat.
Bluff: The sturdy, blunt, near-upright construction of a craft, normally relating to the bows.
Butty: Non-powered boat of a working pair, on the narrow canals. Originally a horse boat but later towed by a motorboat.
Cabin block: Wedge-shaped block on the stern cabin roof of a narrowboat. Used to support the rearmost of a set of top planks.
Carvel build: The construction of a wooden boat with planks laid edge to edge.
Chalico: Protective dressing of horse dung, tar and cow-hair, used in boat building.
Clinker build: The construction of a wooden craft with overlapping side planks.
Cockpit: Open space at the rear of a narrowboat's stern cabin.
Counter: Flat, rounded stern deck of a motorboat.
Counter stern: Raised and rounded stern of a boat or ship.
Cratch: Triangular front board on a narrowboat.

Day boat: Also known as a Joey boat. A boat often used for day trips, sometimes without a stern cabin.

Deck lid: Hinged cover over a locker, at deck level.

Elum or Ellum: Combined rudder and tiller of a butty boat.

Engine hole: Engine-room space on a motorboat.

Fall: Gear for lowering tackle.

Family boat: Boat or barge occupied by the skipper and his family.

Fender: Protective pad or buffer of ropework, hung over the side of a boat to protect it from grazing itself or other surfaces.

Fly boat: A swiftly moving canal boat carrying priority cargoes.

Fore: The front or forward part of a boat.

Forestay: Rope or wire securing a mast or upright at the front. Connects masthead and stem post.

Gaffsail: Sail supported by a spar or gaff in its upper parts.

Gunwale: The upper line or edge, along the hull, of a boat or ship.

Hatches: (1) Covers over a cargo space or the entry to a cabin. (2) Rear entrance to the stern cabin of a narrowboat.

Hold: Cargo space below deck level.

Horse boat: (1) Narrowboat drawn by a horse or other animal. (2) A pontoon or ferry to take horses across a river where there are no bridges and the towing path changes sides.

Jebus: The false bows attached to the first boat in a train of tub boats.

Keelson: An inner keel, fitting above or in place of the keel.

Lateen sail: Triangular sail, attached to a long yard or diagonal with a shorter mast. The mast is stepped well forward, frequently having a short boom at the rear.

Monkey boat: Slang term for a typical narrowboat.

Narrow canals: Narrow-gauge canals with restrictions of navigation at stop-locks to boats of less than 70 feet by 7 feet.

Navigation lamp: Oil or electric lamp displayed on or near the cratch of a narrowboat. Used for night work or in tunnels.

Number one: An owner-boater, mainly on the narrow canals.

Oakum: Lengths of shredded rope used with pitch to seal apertures between planks and such like.

Packet boat: Boat used in regular service for passengers, their hand luggage and small parcels.

Pigeon box: Oblong or box-shaped ventilator above the engine-hole hatch of a motorboat.

Rodney boat: A neglected family boat with scratched paint and dull brasses. A floating slum.

Running blocks: Wooden blocks used to guide a towing rope.

Scouring: Clearing out a canal or navigation to improve its use and appearance.

Shafting: Punting or poling a boat.

Shearings: Panels or planks lining the interior bodywork of a craft.

Side cloths: Protective covers drawn up or let down from the sides of a boat or barge to protect the cargo.

Slack boards: Side planks, also known as wash boards, used to prevent part of a cargo of slack or small coal from slipping into the water.

Slide: Hatch cover on the top of a stern cabin. Made to open by sliding backwards and forwards.

Staithe: Loading gantry, usually at or near a colliery, for loading coal into boats or ships.

Stands: Flattened or attenuated uprights of a narrowboat, supporting top planks and side cloths.

Starvationer: Narrow cigar-shaped boat, formerly used in the underground workings of collieries owned by the Duke of Bridgewater at Worsley near Manchester.

Strakes: Protective horizontal bars or bands protecting the sides, bow and stern of a boat or barge.

Stretcher: (1) Crossbar to which the tow rope is attached for horse towing. (2) Cross plank or bar used to strengthen the hull of a narrowboat.

Struts: Inward-sloping wooden stays used to support the top planks and covers of a narrowboat.

Swan's neck: Ornamental ropework on a butty, connecting the rudder blade with the top of the rudder post or ram's head.

Swim-end: Boat or barge with a flattened, square end (bow or stern) raked to overhang the water at an angle of about 45 degrees.

Swingletree: A later and sturdier form of towing stretcher.

Tiller: Wooden or metal beam attached to the rudder post of a craft for steering.

Top planks: Gangway of planks down the length of the hold or cargo space of a narrowboat. Supported by stands and mast, between cabin roof and cratch.

Towing path: Also known as the haling path or way. Canal or riverside paths used for towing from.

Towing post: The box mast of a boat or barge used for towing.

Transom: A flat, often D-shaped panel forming the stern of certain types of wooden craft.

Tumblehome: Inward-sloping sides of a stern cabin on a narrowboat. More pronounced on a butty or horse boat than on a motorboat or tug.

Tunnel cutter: Metal ring fitted above or across the top of a funnel or stovepipe. This prevents soot or grit from entering the pipe when passing through a tunnel, and also helps to disperse smoke.

Tunnel lamp: Original type of navigation lamp, fixed to the cratch of a narrowboat. Made with either a straight or a curved lens. Eventually replaced by an electric lamp of the van type.

Turk's head: Spliced and woven ropework decorating the top of the rudder post on a butty. This resembled the turban of a Turkish warrior.

Una rig: A type of rig popular on the east coast and waterways of East Anglia. It consisted of a large single sail with gaff and boom, the mast stepped well forward. Any craft with una rig is fairly shallow and broad in the beam, often fitted with an extra keel or centre board.

Waterman: Boatman or bargee, usually working on a river rather than a canal navigation.

Windlass: (1) Gear for raising heavy loads. (2) An L-shaped tool used for opening the paddles on lock gates. Often carried in the waist band or belt of a boater.

Windlass hole: Cupboard in the stern cabin of a narrowboat where a spare windlass of the type used for opening locks was kept.

Bibliography

Aickman, Robert. *Know Your Waterways*. Sir Isaac Pitman, 1955.

Austed, A. *A Dictionary of Sea Terms*. L. Upcott Gill, 1898.

Baldwin, Mark, and Burton, Anthony. *Canals, A New Look.* Phillimore, 1984.

Chaplin, Tom. *The Narrow Boat Book*. Whittel Books, reprinted 1984.

De Mare, Eric. *The Canals of England*. Architectural Press, 1955.

De Salis, H. R. *Bradshaw's Guide to the Canals and Navigable Rivers of England*. H. Blucklock, 1904. Reprinted, David and Charles, 1966.

Fairfax, B. *Walking London Waterways*. David and Charles, 1985.

Gagg, John. *The Observer's Book of Canals*. Frederick Warne, 1982.

Hadfield, Charles. *British Canals*. David and Charles, 1966.

Hazell, Martin. *Sailing Barges*. Shire Publications, second edition reprinted 1986.

Le Fleming, H. M. *ABC of Coastal Passenger Shipping*. Ian Allan.

Lewery, A. J. *Narrow Boat Painting*. David and Charles, 1974.

Malet, Hugh. *Voyage in a Bowler Hat*. M. Baldwin, 1985.

Paget-Tomlinson, Edward W. *The Complete Book of Canal and River Navigations*. Waine Research Publications, 1978.

Rolt, L. T. C. *Narrow Boat*. Eyre and Spottiswoode, 1944.

Smith, D. J. *Canal Boats and Boaters*. Hugh Evelyn, 1973.

Smith, Peter L. *Canal Barges and Narrowboats*. Shire Publications, fourth edition 1986.

Stammers, M. K. *Steamboats*. Shire Publications, 1986.

Stammers, M. K. *Historic Ships*. Shire Publications, 1987.

Useful information may also be obtained from *Waterways World,* a monthly magazine published by Waterway Productions Limited, Kottingham House, Dale Street, Burton-upon-Trent, Staffordshire, DE14 3TD (available through all newsagents).

Places to visit

Bewdley Museum, The Shambles, Load Street, Bewdley, Worcestershire. Telephone: Bewdley (0299) 403573. Items and models relating to the Severn navigation and trows.

Black Country Museum, Tipton Road, Dudley, West Midlands DY1 4SQ. Telephone: 021-557 9643. Canal craft, basin and repair yard. Trips through canal tunnel.

Blake's Lock Museum, Gasworks Road (off Kenavon Drive), Reading, Berkshire. Telephone: Reading (0734) 590630. The development of local waterways.

Blists Hill Open Air Museum, Coalport Road, Madeley, Telford, Shropshire. Telephone: Telford (0952) 586063 or 583003.

The Boat Museum, Dockyard Road, Ellesmere Port, Cheshire L65 4EF. Telephone: 051-355 5017. Access from junction 9 of M53. A working museum in docks shared by the Shropshire Union Canal and the Manchester Ship Canal. Over fifty historic canal boats, barges and other craft, and exhibitions about canal life.

Bristol Industrial Museum, Prince's Wharf, Prince Street, Bristol BS1 4RN. Telephone: Bristol (0272) 299771. Collection of transport items dealing with land, sea and inland navigation. Also items connected with the port of Bristol, such as models of Severn trows.

Canal Exhibition, Canal Wharf, Whaley Bridge, Stockport, Cheshire. Telephone: Whaley Bridge (066 33) 3411.

Canal Exhibition, Plus Pleasures Marine, The Clock Warehouse, London Road, Shardlow, Derbyshire. Telephone: Derby (0332) 792844.

Canal Museum, Canal Street, Nottingham. Telephone: Nottingham (0602) 598835. General exhibition of craft, bridges and equipment relating to waterways. Based on the site of a former canal warehouse.

Canal Museum, Mill Street East, Dewsbury, West Yorkshire. Telephone: Dewsbury (0924) 467976. (By appointment only.)

Dolphin Sailing Barge Museum, Crown Quay Lane, Sittingbourne, Kent. Telephone: Maidstone (0622) 62531.

Exeter Maritime Museum, The Quay, Exeter, Devon EX2 4AN. Telephone: Exeter (0392) 58075. The world's largest collection of boats, including an example from the Bude Canal and Brunel's canal dredger.

Goole Museum and Art Gallery, Goole Library, Market Square, Carlisle Street, Goole, Humberside DN14 5AA. Telephone: Goole (0405) 2187. Models, prints, paintings and other items relating to the port of Goole and its connecting waterways.

Linlithgow Union Canal Society Museum, Manse Road Basin, Linlithgow, West Lothian. Telephone: Linlithgow (050 684) 4730.

Llangollen Canal Exhibition, The Wharf, Llangollen, Clwyd. Telephone: Llangollen (0978) 860702. Models, displays, artefacts. Horse-drawn boat trips.

Maritime Museum, Old Custom House, St George's Quay, Lancaster. Telephone: Lancaster (0524) 64637. The port of Lancaster and the Lancaster Canal.

Morwellham Quay Open Air Museum, Morwellham, Tavistock, Devon PL19 8JL. Telephone: Tavistok (0822) 832766. Items connected with local navigations and the tub boat canals.

National Maritime Museum, Romney Road, Greenwich, London SE10 9NF. Telephone: 01-858 4422. Many items of interest including a reconstructed Thames-side boatyard, a steam tug from the Manchester Ship Canal Company and the steam inspection launch *Donola,* formerly used on the upper reaches of the Thames.

Newbury District Museum, The Wharf, Newbury, Berkshire RG14 5AS. Telephone: Newbury (0635) 30511. The Kennet and Avon Canal.

Port of Harwich Maritime Museum, The Low Lighthouse, Harwich Green, Harwich, Essex. Telephone: Harwich (0255) 503429. Barge traffic.

St Katharine's Dock, near Tower Bridge, London E1. The typical Thames tug *Challenge* and Thames barges.

Science Museum, Exhibition Road, South Kensington, London SW7 2DD. Telephone: 01-589 3456. Several items and displays, including models, relating to the inland waterways.

Town Docks Museum, Queen Victoria Square, Kingston upon Hull, Humberside HU1 3DX. Telephone: Hull (0482) 222737.

Transport and Archaeology Museum, 36 High Street, Kingston upon Hull, Humberside. Telephone: Hull (0482) 222737. Navigation of the Humber, ships, barges and keels.

Waterways Museum, Stoke Bruerne, Towcester, Northamptonshire. Telephone: Northampton (0604) 862229. Two hundred years of canal history displayed in the form of actual craft, models, artefacts, prints and documents. Privately run boat trips.

Wigan Pier, Wigan, Lancashire WN3 4EU. Telephone: Wigan (0942) 323666. Canalside heritage centre. Waterbus services.

Willis Museum and Art Gallery, Old Town Hall, Market Place, Basingstoke, Hampshire RB21 1QD. Telephone: Basingstoke (0256) 465902. Items relating to the Basingstoke Canal.

Windermere Steamboat Museum, Rayrigg Road, Windermere, Cumbria LA23 1BU. Telephone: Windermere (096 62) 5565.

Index

Aidie 26
Aire and Calder Navigations 31, 32, 68, 72
Albion 29
Ampton boat 64
Ant, river 28
Ashby Canal 70
Aust 78
Avon (Bristol) 55, 57
Avon (Warwickshire) 75
Avon tar barge 57

Bacat 79
Barbara Jean 26
Barge 7, 8, 19-26
Barlow boat 65
Bartholomew, W. H. 31, 32
Basingstoke Canal 26
Bath 69
Bawley 16, plate 6
Beachley 78
Best boat 13, 14
Bewdley 55, 59
Birmingham 64, 65
Birmingham Canal Navigations 32, 60, 63, 64, 66
Blue top 66
Bonapart 70
Boston 69
Box trow 56
Bradford-on-Avon 69
Bridgewater, Duke of 59, 70
Bridgewater Canal 59, 64, 69, 70, 71, 74
Bridgwater and Taunton Canal 73
Brighouse 30
Brightlingsea 26
Brindley, James 59
Bristol 55
Bristol Channel 55, 56, 57
Brunel, Isambard K. 72
Bude Canal 68
Bure 28
Butty 60, 62

Cabin cruiser 76
Calder and Hebble Navigation 30, 81
Canoe 5, 18, 19
Captain's gig 12
Cardiff 57
Carvel build 4, 5
Chain ferry 78
Chalk barge 22, 23
Charlotte Dundas 69, 70
Clayton, Joshua 64
Clinker build 4, 5
Clinker eight 11
Clinker four 11
Clyde 50, 52, 75
Coaching gig 12
Coal gabbart 50
College barge 7, 8, 9, plate 2
Compartment boats 31, 32, 72, 78, 79
Coracle 4, 6
Crinan Canal 50
Curragh, Irish 5-6

Cyclops 52

Dart 75, 76, 77
Day boat 63, plate 18
Dee 6, 75
De Salis, H. R. 74
Diesel-powered narrowboat 60
Dinghy 16, 17
Doggett's Coat and Badge 8, 9
Doncaster 80
Donola 80
Dredgers 72-3
Droitwich Canal 55
Duchess-Countess type 59
Duck punt 17-18
Dugout 3, 5
Dumb barge 19, 53, 54, 58, 70, 73
Dummy bows 32

East Cowes 78
Edgar, King 7
Eight-oared boats 9, 10, 11
Eight-oared shell 10
Ellesmere, Earl of 74
Ellesmere Port, Boat Museum 66
Eton College 10
Eton skiff 12
Excavator dredger 72
Exeter Maritime Museum 73

Family boat 60-1
Fellows Morton & Clayton 64, 66, 74
Ferries 77-8, plate 22
Ferrybridge 78
Fly boat 60, 68
FMC boats 64-5
Forth and Clyde Canal 51, 52, 69, 70
Funny 14, 15

Gainsborough 49
Gas boat 66
General-service boats 73-4
Gifford 66
Gig 8, 11, 12
Gloucester 57, 59, 71
Gloucester and Sharpness Canal 55, 57, 58, 69, 71
Goole 30, 31, 32, 69, 78
Grand Junction Canal 66, 71
Grand Union Canal 65-6, 71, 74
Grand Western Canal 68
Gravesend 22, 78
Guildford 26
Gun punt 17-18

Hand-propelled craft 10-19
Harecastle Tunnel 72
Henley-on-Thames 10
Hoy 15
Hull 30, 31, 78
Humber 29, 30, 49, 59, 78
Humber keel 29-31, 49, plate 13

Icebreaker 72, 73
Inspection boats and launches 74-5

Ironbridge 6
Irwell 52

Jebus 32
Joey boat 63
Joshers 60, 62, 64

Keadby 49
Kennet and Avon Canal 57, 67
Kingston-upon-Thames 75
Kingswear 78

Lady Hatherton 74
Lash system 79
Leeds 32, 69
Leeds and Liverpool Canal 53, 54, 55, 59
Leigh 55
Lighter 19, 21
Limehouse 71
Lincoln 69
Lincoln Castle 78
Linda 66
Little packets 71
Lomond, Loch 75
London 7, 9, 19, 22, 26, 65, 69, 71
Long boat (hand-propelled) 15
Long boat (narrowboat) 59
Lord Dundas
Lord Roberts 29
Lower Avon Navigation 72
Lowestoft 28
Luff barge 24

Maid of the Loch 75
Manchester 59, 71, 74
Medina 78
Medway 16, 19, 22, 23, 24
Medway doble 16, plate 4
Mersey 52, 53, 59, 78
Mersey flat 52-3
Mew 78
Monk, Thomas 59
Monkey boat 59
Monro, Neil 52
Mulberry Harbour 17

Narrowboats 59-67, plates 18-20
Newark-on-Trent 49
New Holland 78
Newport 57
Norfolk keel 27, plate 11
Norfolk wherry 13, 27, 28-9, plate 12
Norman, John 8
Norwich 27, 29
Nottingham 49

Oldbury 66
Ouse (Yorkshire) 29, 30, 49
Outrigger pair 11
Outrigger scull 11
Oxford 7, 9, 10, 22, 75
Oyster skiff 12-13

Packet boats 59, 68-9
Peter-boat 15, plate 5

INDEX

Pioneer 70
Pleasure punt 17
Pleasure steamer 75
Pleasure wherry 8
Pontoon 16-17, 77, plate 10
Private barge 8
Puffer 50-2
Punt 5, 17, plate 7
Putney 10

Racing boats 10, 11
Racing punt 17
Raft 5
Randan 13-14
Regent's Canal 69, 71
Rickmansworth 65
Ricky boat 65
River class 66
Rocking boat 73
Rodney boat 62
Rolt, L.T.C. 76
Rough punt 17
Royalty class 65
Rum-tum 14
Runcorn 59, 70, 71
Runcorn boat 64

Sailing barge 19-26, 28, plates 8, 9
Salter Brothers 75
Saul 57
Scow 77
Sculls 11
Semi-racer 17
Severn 6, 55, 57, 59, 72, 75, 78
Severn and Thames Canal 72
Severn King 78
Severn tanker 57
Severn trow 55-7, plate 17
Sharpness 71
Sharpness (tug) 71, 72
Sheffield and South Yorkshire Canal 31, 49
Shell 10, 13

Short boat 53-5
Shortwood 72
Shrewsbury 6, 55
Shroppie fly 64
Shropshire Union Canal 59, 64
Skiff 8, 9, 12, 77
Skinboat 5, 6
Spoon dredger 72
Spritsail barge 23, 24, 25, plate 8
Stackie barge 26
Staffordshire and Worcestershire Canal 72, 74
Star class 65
Starvationer 59
State barge 7-9, plate 1
Steam narrowboat 66-7
Stourport-on-Severn 55, 56, 57
Stroudwater barge 57
Stroudwater Navigation 55, 57
Stumpy barge 26
Swim-headed barge 20, 22
Swimmie 20
Swinton 31

Tardebigge 72
Taylor, Matthew 10
Teifi 6
Teign 58
Teignmouth keel 58
Ten-oared boat 9
Thames 7, 8, 9, 10, 12, 14, 15, 16, 19, 20, 22, 23, 24, 26, 59, 65, 73, 75, 78
Thames sailing barge 19-26, plates 8, 9
Thames skiff 12
Thames wherry 8, 13, 29, plate 3
Tom puddings 31-2, 49, 68, 72, plate 14
Torrington Canal 68
Town class 65
Towy 6
Trent and Mersey Canal 72

Trent barge 49, plate 15
Trent Navigation 49
Trevithick, Richard 73
Trow 18
Tub boats 68, 80
Tugs 31, 70-2, 79, 80, plates 21, 23
Tyne 18, 49
Tyne keel 49-50, plate 16
Tyne wherry 50

University Boat Race 10

Wager boat 13, 14
Wakefield 32
Waveney 28
Weaver 52, 53
Weaver flat 52-3
Weaver steam flat 51, 53
Welsh narrowboat 67
West country vessel 30
Western barge 20, 22
Wey barge 26
Wey Navigation 26
Wherry 8, 13, 77
Whiff 13
Whiff gig 13
Wich barge 55
William 56
Wonder 29
Woolwich ferry 78
Worcester 57
Worcester and Birmingham Canal 72
Work flat 73-4
Working pair 61-3
Worsley 59, 70
Wye 6

Yare 27, 28, 78
Yarmouth 28
York 30
Yorkshire keel 29, 30, 49

Printed in Great Britain by C. I. Thomas & Sons (Haverfordwest) Ltd, Press Buildings, Merlins Bridge, Haverfordwest, Dyfed.